What People Are Saying About

Paranormal Perspectives:
A Jungian Understanding of Transcendent Experiences

A moving, gut-honest memoir of the author's experiences on her journey of spiritual awakening. Ms. Plunket expertly describes and leads us into the myriad of disillusionments, confusion, breakthroughs and thrills that frequently arise on the authentic pathway of self-discovery. Readers will undoubtedly identify with both the pain and triumph of transcending the confines of personality and ego.
Carole J. Obley, author, *Wisdom from the Spirit World*

If you've ever asked, What am I doing here? What is my purpose? What is my soul's journey? Does evil exist? this is the book for you.

Susan Plunket weaves together psychological insight and soul wisdom to take you on a journey into multidimensional reality to answer these very questions. It's a brave telling exposing both her failures and breakthroughs as she attempts to demolish her imperial ego.

But it's far more than her own story of awakening, captivating as that is. It's a guide for awakening your own divine power, a book to be cherished and shared with all those you love.
Dr. Sura Al-Shibib, intuitive chiropractor

This is literally a 19-chapter guidebook for life in which Susan Plunket shares how her journey has been guided by spiritual teachers and guides from other dimensions

T0182503

Susan's writing is ethereal and vulnerable as she recounts the experiences from early childhood to mature womanhood that shaped her life, allowing us also to benefit from them.

At the same time, it's down-to-earth and practical, a book which I will refer to for years to come. I know I will continue to gain additional layers of understanding and wisdom from Susan's teachers and guides, and to regularly revisit the exercises at the end of each chapter.

Throughout the book, I felt Susan's desire to enhance the lives of all of us as she encourages us to trust the spiritual path our lives take and to know, beyond a doubt, that we are loved and supported through our highest pinnacles and the deepest valleys.

I was particularly moved by how Susan shared her adult insights around her early childhood experiences. As she does this, she reminds us how the cycle of life allows us to spiral back through time to gain a deeper understanding of our younger self.

I highly recommend Susan's book to all seekers open to receiving metaphysical guidance and insight through dreams, symbols, ancient wisdom and paranormal experiences.

Jo-Anne Brown, author, intuitive healer

Welcome to Paranormal Perspectives

It was important for me to develop Paranormal Perspectives for those seeking a deeper understanding of the paranormal world. This series is intended for sceptics, believers, and those who have unfathomable experiences and are often frightened by them. These books will help their understanding of what is happening to them.

The Paranormal Perspectives series will explore, in-depth, the encounters, theories, and research into incomprehensible events and how these experiences motivated remarkable individuals to delve deeper and share their extraordinary relationships of the paranormal with the world.

Paranormal Perspectives begins with five books exploring the spectrum of metaphysical events, with insight from the UK's top ghost detective, a licensed clinical psychologist, a retired English professor, a prolific UFO investigator, and a writer specialising in first-hand, personal paranormal encounters.

You, too, may have had a lifetime of unearthly experiences and may wish to add to the series. Please visit 6th-books.com for further information. We look forward to hearing from you.

I hope you enjoy this series as it guides you on your quest and pulls back the veil to shine light into the unknown.

Sleep well,

G L Davies

Author of *Haunted: Horror of Haverfordwest*

Paranormal Perspectives

One Big Box of 'Paranormal Tricks': From Ghosts to Poltergeists to the Theory of Just One Paranormal Power
by John Fraser

A Jungian Understanding of Transcendent Experiences
by Susan Plunket

Hauntings, Attachments and Ghouls
by G L Davies

Portraits of Alien Encounters Revisited
by Nigel Harry Watson

Where the Spirit Led
by Brad Burkholder

Paranormal Perspectives: A Jungian Understanding of Transcendent Experiences

Paranormal Perspectives: A Jungian Understanding of Transcendent Experiences

Susan Plunket

6TH
BOOKS

Winchester, UK
Washington, USA

CollectiveInk

First published by Sixth Books, 2024
Sixth Books is an imprint of Collective Ink Ltd.,
Unit 11, Shepperton House, 89 Shepperton Road, London, N1 3DF
office@collectiveinkbooks.com
www.collectiveinkbooks.com
www.6th-books.com

For distributor details and how to order please visit the 'Ordering' section on our website.

Text copyright: Susan Plunket 2023

ISBN: 978 1 80341 523 9
978 1 80341 526 0 (ebook)
Library of Congress Control Number: 2023933906

A CIP catalogue record for this book is available from the British Library.

Design: Lapiz Digital Services

UK: Printed and bound by CPI Group (UK) Ltd, Croydon, CR0 4YY
Printed in North America by CPI GPS partners

We operate a distinctive and ethical publishing philosophy in all areas of our business, from our global network of authors to production and worldwide distribution.

Other Titles by This Author

When Every Breath Becomes a Prayer
978-0985715250

Mission from Venus
978-1789041705

The Wanderers on Earth
978-1789045321

Contents

Chapter 1

Phantom Twin

In the world of humans, the year is 1947. A lot of beings on planet Earth are still recovering from a big war. I'm not sure this is the right time to incarnate, but my guides remind me of the agreements I've made. Fortunately, I'm not incarnating alone but with a twin, Sophie. For several months we've been coming and going to and from the Earth plane preparing the bodies we will inhabit. We're creating not only our baby bodies but also what they will become. These bodies are our idea of ourselves in material form. Using the vibration of love we create the photons to make our bodies. Photons are the building blocks for everything material. First we worked with our idea of our physical selves, because physical bodies can't exist unless they are first an idea, a thought. Only once an idea creates a vibration can something manifest in the physical realm.

Right now we're in the formless realm, about to return to the mother's body on Earth. Sophie hesitates then telegraphs to me that she's not coming with me. She's changed her mind. She's afraid of being born into the Third Dimension. She reminds me that being born is much harder than dying and she can't face the shock of it. I'm frightened of the Third Dimension too. I know great masters who fear to cover their light in flesh. I'm sad that Sophie isn't coming with me. I hesitate, but for some reason I go back in the ninth month of the mother's pregnancy and stay to be born alone without Sophie. Maybe I do it because I know and love the Soul who is to be my human father. I have an agreement with him to be his daughter in this life. I share other lives with him in other galaxies. Sophie reminds me that I will forget who he is once I'm born and that I will even forget who I am, my true Self.

Sophie was right. It was a huge shock to be born. Everyone thinks I can't understand anything because I'm in a helpless small body which I can't yet operate very well. Everything they give me to drink hurts my insides. I get energy from the other realm and some through breathing. My parents don't understand this. They have forgotten because they've been here so long. They seem unaware of their subtle bodies. I cry a lot and my mother doesn't know what to do with me. I also have lots of allergies. The worst is itchy eczema all over my baby body. My mother ties my wrists to the crib bars so I can't scratch myself.

The decision to incarnate on Earth feels like a mistake. I leave my baby body often and go to the other side to visit. My guides encourage me to stay on Earth assuring me that I will learn a lot. They remind me that every Soul born on Earth not only comes here to learn but also brings a unique gift. They also remind me that I made an agreement with those in the formless realm to fulfill a task. I no longer remember what that is. I lost a lot of my greater Self while passing through the veil of forgetting. It's a condition of life on Earth that all beings must pass through the veil and forget who they are and all their other lives. I think this law is peculiar to life on Earth. When I leave the baby's body I sometimes visit myself in other existences. In this life on Earth my human mother and father call me Susan, but Sophie knows me as Soonam, which is my Soul name.

I've been here for two years now. I just got another big shock. I learned that since I'm two I'm no longer permitted to leave the baby's body and return to the other side to stay, though I can still visit. The longer I'm here, the more I forget. My eyes and ears and whole body feel designed to tune into this life on Earth, almost forcing me to experience only it. Even though I still know that many other dimensions open onto this one, the windows to those worlds are closing except for when my human body is sleeping.

Sophie just arrived to visit me.

"I thought this would always be an option," I communicate to her telepathically. "I mean to leave if it was too hard being in a physical body."

She understands how I feel. "Now you have to stay in the space/time world," she says sadly.

We have a fenced in back yard where I play and make mud cakes for the fairies and elves and gnomes. My mother leaves me out here and goes in the house to do the laundry, make the beds, and drink coffee and talk on the telephone. But I am never alone. There are small beings among the flowers. I tell Sophie I am forgetting where I came from. I am forgetting what God is like. She tries to help by reminding me that God doesn't only look one way and he didn't only create Earth. He is an infinite field of consciousness. He is everything. He created endless universes. He takes many forms based on the beliefs of the beings inhabiting those universes. Sophie points to a spider crawling on a flowerpot.

"God is that spider too, just as God is you and me and the flowerpot. God is an endless fountain of light supporting us all."

She reminds me I am also living other lives right now, that only a part of me is on Earth. I'm happy when she tells me that we're together right now in the Pleiades serving as temple goddesses. What she means is that other parts of our Over Souls are living other existences simultaneously as I live this one on Earth. I nearly forgot this though I have seen us living other lives in my dreams. I don't want to forget, but forgetfulness is creeping over me, burying me like overgrown vines encasing a castle. I tell her, telepathically, that I remember another dream where I am sitting in council in the formless realm. In council we are telepathically discussing how to convey to humans the mastery of sound so they can use it for healing and for moving heavy physical matter. I tell Sophie I'm more confused the longer I'm here. I ask her if my dream is real. She assures me it is more real than this life I'm living on Earth which is a big camouflage.

When Sophie's with me I have to look out for her so someone doesn't sit on her or shut the car door on her. My mother tells me to stop imaging things and talking nonsense. My father says to let them know when Sophie is with me so they won't bump into her or put things down on top of her. Every day my father goes to work at the high school where he coaches and teaches gym classes. I don't like it when he leaves unless Sophie is with me. She comes to help me keep my connection to the eternal world. Today she told me to try and be aware that I'm using the energy of my thoughts not only to make my body grow but to create everything I see.

"Every moment your thoughts are creating changes in your body and in the physical world."

I'm not aware of this, I tell her.

"You're doing it unconsciously," she says. "You work below the level of consciousness with all the other humans to sustain the illusion of the physical world you experience and your own physical body too. Most humans have no idea how powerful they are or even what they are. Try to use your inner senses while you're awake. Babies and small children still have clairvoyance and telepathy. They still belong to the eternal world. You will lose your connection to the eternal world the longer you're on Earth unless you practice tuning into your inner senses."

I'm sad when she says this. I will try harder to not lose my connection to the eternal world. She says that "everyone when they're first born knows the eternal timeless world, but the longer they're on Earth the more they become hypnotized by the external world of space and time. The split between the two worlds becomes a gulf more and more difficult to bridge. By adulthood the eternal world is mostly out of reach. Try not to let that happen to you. Keep a foot in both worlds for as long as you can. Keep your eternal being alive inside your human self. Live both of yourselves."

When she says goodbye, I cry inside my head.

Exercise: Your Eternal Self

Lie down and close your eyes. Make your body comfortable. Notice any pain, contraction or discomfort. Imagine spirals of light coming in through the soles of your feet and flowing up to soothe any discomfort you feel. Check to make sure you're breathing through your nose, not your mouth. With each gentle inhale imagine more light spirals entering through the soles of your feet. Ask your body to release any tension. Our bodies listen when we talk to them. Every organ and every cell and even every atom in us is conscious and listening to our messages.

Bring your mind's eye now to the center of your heart and see a door opening into a garden. All your favorite trees and flowers are growing in this garden. Maybe there is a brook or a pond or a fountain. In your garden you will find your eternal timeless Self, waiting for you. Look around for her. She may be standing beside your tree of life or perhaps seated on a bench. Approach her. She knows more about you than anyone and she will help you with anything you ask. Ask her a question if you feel like it. Then listen.

Chapter 2

The Question

I'm six years old and I have a three-year-old brother. I'm in first grade. Dwight Eisenhower is our president. His photograph is up on our bulletin board at school. My teacher, Miss McGinnis, says he's a war hero. I like to sit near the windows so I can look up into the sky.

Miss McGinnis moved my desk to the other side of the room near the bulletin board. This morning we subtracted tomatoes from tomatoes to see how many tomatoes were left. Now we're working on writing the alphabet in capital and small letters. Miss McGinnis is walking up and down the aisles checking our work. She leans over my desk to make sure I'm printing on the lines with the big fat green pencil. I look up and ask her what we're all doing here on Earth.

"Aren't you a Christian?" she says with surprise.

I don't know why she said that. What does being a Christian have to do with why we're here? What I know so far about church is that they tell you have to be good so the devil doesn't get you. Church feels dead. What do they mean, "I'll put the fear of God in you"? God isn't scary. What I want to know is why I'm on Earth, why I came here and if I'll ever see God again. I don't know how to find out, who I can ask. Not my mother. I'm afraid of her. Maybe my father. Or maybe I'll ask God and see if I hear anything back.

We have a small room next to our kitchen. It's called a pantry. There is a bushel of apples in there. They smell so sweet. I like to close the door and sit on the floor next to them. They're good company.

Something nice happened. My grandfather bought us a television. It gets three channels. I want to know how it works.

Faraway people come right into our living room through it, like they do in a dream. It seems like magic except there's no color, everything is only black and white. I add color in my mind. My father turns it on. I see a fairy princess. While we watch my father explains that the princess is being crowned as Queen Elizabeth because her father the King died. I squeeze my father's hand.

This world on Earth is taking over my mind more and more. I hardly remember anything from before. I still visit my home in the other world when my body is asleep even though I can't stay. In that world I don't have to use words. We just know what each other is thinking and feeling. And there I create everything instantly with my thoughts. My guardian angel told me I'm creating things on Earth too using love to make light. It's love that creates photons, she says. I feel small and scared here a lot. I ask her why I'm on Earth. She says I must discover that myself.

We have an apple tree in our yard. I lean against it and look up into its branches and ask it, "What am I doing here? Do you know? I have been here for six years. Why don't I belong?"

The wind stirs the apple blossoms and they fall down on me like little kisses. I thank them. They appreciate that. We're made of the same stuff so I can understand them. There is energy inside everything, even in the nails my father is using to build shelves in our garage. I say hello to the nails.

It's summer. No more school. My father is teaching my brother and me how to swim. We hold onto the dock and practice flutter kicks. I like those words. Flutter kicks. He tells us to put our faces in the water and blow bubbles. I like the smell of the snack bar near the lake. The cement floor gets wet from kids' bathing suits dripping on it while they wait for their turn to buy popsicles and fudgesicles and frozen Milky Way bars.

A white-haired lady my mother knows gave me a whole set of books called *The Little Colonel*. The little colonel is a girl and she has a horse. I read outside sitting under the apple tree.

Summer is over so fast. Time is funny. It speeds up and jumps ahead or it slows down and stretches out.

I'm in second grade. At school we have drills where we practice getting under our desks in case the Russians drop a nuclear bomb on us. I don't know why they would want to do that.

My mother is screaming and throwing boxes about. She's just come down from the attic. Silverfish ate holes her wedding dress.

"I hate this house," she screams.

I wonder, what are silver fish? How did fish get in our attic? I run outside and hide under the apple tree.

"Our house used to be a barn and the large old beams have silverfish in them," my father tells me later.

It was my grandfather, father to my father, who turned the barn into a house for us. He died soon after he and his men finished it. He was sixty-two. When my grandfather died my father had to sleep sitting up so he could breathe. After my grandfather died I saw my father talking to him. They were standing together in our garden next to the lettuce.

Today my father was organizing his desk and he showed me a photograph of the car his father bought him when he was in college so he could come home to visit. It was brown and white like my saddle shoes. I ask him if his father still comes to visit him. He smiles at me.

I have to see the school psychologist because I did something wrong. I don't know what. My mother is angry at me. She told my father I'm a "trial." I don't know what that is. But I know it's bad.

I sit across a big desk which is level with my chin and listen as the psychologist tells me I have to take the IQ test again because I didn't answer the questions. He shows me my answer sheet.

"It looks like instead of answering the questions by filling in the spaces between the lines to choose your answer for each question you just made a pattern."

He asks me why I did this. I don't know. He gives me some red and white blocks and tells me to copy the designs he shows me. I enjoy this. He smiles at me. Maybe I'm not bad. After we finish the psychologist walks me back to my classroom. I know everyone will look at me when I walk in because I had to see the school psychologist. I try to think of a song to feel better. My mother puts on a record when she wants to feel good. She says music lifts her spirit.

I sing "Hound Dog" inside my head.

Exercise: Self-Acceptance

If a fear or a mood or an angry feeling or a self-judgement, or a judgement of someone else, catches hold of you and you become aware of it, that's good. You observed your state. Observing yourself, catching yourself in the act of judgement is the hardest thing. Too many times we push the cup of honesty away because the truth is too bitter. But the task is to witness the mind, to see all the things we might not like about ourselves, our fears, our meanness, jealousy, coldness.

Once you observe something in yourself you can change it. The first step is welcome. Welcome is a change maker, an alchemical process. Begin by welcoming even your meanness and your fears. Accept them all with open arms like they're old friends. Give them a good warm welcome. Welcome even your envy and self-hatred as friends, as you accept them as part of you they'll begin to transform and loosen their grip on you. The warmer your welcome the faster they will dissolve. Your acceptance is the magic which dissolves them.

Chapter 3

Flying Saucer over the Ashokan Reservoir

I'm eleven. Besides my brother I now have a six-year-old sister and a little two-year-old brother. We live on top of Bostock Mountain in a white house. A few miles down the mountain, and along a winding country road bordered with orange tiger lilies in summer, is the Ashokan Reservoir. Ashokan is a Native American word. It means "place of fish." The reservoir was constructed between 1907 and 1912 to hold water for New York City. I know this because I wrote a paper on it for school.

My father is now the high school principal, though I think he misses coaching. My mother is a hospital administrator at Kingston Hospital, a job she loves. Money is less of a problem than it was when I was little. We moved from Phoenicia and the house my grandfather built to Shokan and my mother now has the house of her dreams.

I'm still a little afraid of her. I want her to like me. Today I picked lilacs and put them in a vase and brought them to her.

"They bring in bugs, take them outside," she said.

There is energy and sweetness in them she doesn't sense because she uses her nose and eyes too much instead of her inner senses. She's hurt their feelings by not welcoming them. She likes flowers from the florist but I don't have any money.

Even though I'm eleven I still have a lot of nightmares about a creature with scales chasing me and trying to kill me. Sometimes my father comes to comfort me. He tells me to think of having a picnic under a big leafy tree on a beautiful summer day.

"Always keep something beautiful in your mind," he says.

My grandfather still visits my father in his dreams and sometimes when he's awake too. He comes and stands near my father and they talk without words, just using their minds. I want to ask if my grandfather is with God, but I don't. I have seen my father kneeling by his bed talking to God. If my mother does this, I don't see her. My father says she feels betrayed by God because both her parents were killed in an accident when she was a small child and she had to be raised by a strict aunt. I want to say, God doesn't betray anyone. Sophie told me one of the last times I saw her that we choose the things that happen to us to help us grow, before we even come here. But I keep quiet. I like to work in the garden with my father. My mother never comes there.

I'm falling asleep and I hear voices calling my name. "Who's there?" I ask the air. "Are you the nymphs and fairies from our garden?"

I drift off.

I'm floating above the reservoir near a flying saucer. My six-year-old sister, Anne, is floating beside me. The flying saucer is hovering but it doesn't land. Then suddenly it isn't there anymore and the sky above the reservoir is empty. I look at Anne who says into my mind without speaking that she's seen this flying saucer here before.

Then we're out in space near the moon looking at it. I don't know how we got here. Anne reads my mind.

"We imagined ourselves here," she says. "If you imagine it, it happens. That's how you move from place to place when your body is asleep. You don't use your will. Imagination works better."

Anne still remembers more than I do how things work because she hasn't been here as long. Her brain waves haven't changed yet. Earth is very beautiful below us. We float for a while gazing at the moon. It looks reddish. Then suddenly we're back in our room looking down at our bodies which wait for us in our beds. They don't know we're not in them.

When I wake up the next morning Anne has her face pressed against our mirror.

"What are you doing?" I ask her.

"I'm looking at the white part of my eyes to see my spirit like my angel told me."

At breakfast Anne tells our mother we visited the moon. I know better than to share this information with my mother, but Anne is only six. My mother tells her to stop making up stories. I overhear my mother say to my father that she's worried about Anne saying weird things in school. "She's in first grade now. This has got to stop. I don't want her to turn out like Susan, with her head in the clouds."

My father tells her he had remote viewing ability as a child too and it's nothing to worry about. It's a gift.

I did something careless and stupid. I froze my feet ice skating. The town of Woodstock made a skating rink on the field across from the cemetery. It was below zero the day I did it. A voice in my head said to put on an extra pair of wool socks before lacing up my skates. It wasn't like me to have such a practical idea. I wondered whose voice said that. My skates were tight with the extra socks but I was having fun so I stayed on and on for hours twirling around and around on the ice without realizing I couldn't feel my feet. When I got home and took off my socks, my toes were as black as coal. I showed my mother. She screamed.

My parents each took one foot between their palms and rubbed my black toes. It started to hurt. I stared across the room at the fire in the fireplace. My father took off his belt and put the leather between my teeth. "Bite," he said. My mother wanted to take me to the hospital in Kingston. "They may have to amputate her toes to prevent gangrene," she said to my father.

I begged my mother not to take me to the hospital to get my toes cut off. For once she listened to me, though she threatened that it could be more than my toes I would lose if we waited. It could be my feet and maybe my legs if gangrene set in. I don't know what gangrene is.

My father said, "We'll keep massaging. It will take too long to get to the hospital. We'd lose precious time."

Slowly the black gave way to patches of bluish white. After I don't know how long, maybe half an hour, my toes were a cold bluish-white color and they still looked pretty dead. My father carried me to bed and covered me up. He leaned down and kissed my forehead.

I feel sad. How will I manage without toes? How will I do the bunny hop when I'm old enough to go to school dances? I try to sleep but each time I doze, I jerk awake and see a large reptile standing upright next to my bed, grinning. The next second it turns into a man, then back to a reptile again. I freeze in terror. I can't even scream.

By morning my feet are swollen to three times their size. My father carries me to the car and lays me across the back seat. He covers me with a blanket. I see for a moment a child in a barn being nibbled on by rats. A man comes into the barn and lifts the child off the floor and puts her in a horse drawn cart and covers her with a blanket. The man is my father in old-fashioned clothes. I think the child is me. Am I dreaming while awake? Have my frozen toes affected my brain?

The doctor says it's safer to amputate the toes now. Or we could take it a day at a time watching for signs of gangrene but that's risky. I beg to wait. My mother listens to me but reminds me that choices have consequences. When we get home my father places a coffee table in my bed. He turns it on its side with its legs pointing toward me. My mother drapes the sheet and blanket over the table so nothing will touch my feet.

Twice a day my mother examines my feet for signs of gangrene. Each time I hold my breath waiting for the verdict.

I dream of the reptile who is angry and threatening, telling me that I haven't seen the last of him. My father says I must take control of my dreams and tell the reptile to leave, and if he doesn't, I will envelop him with my light. He reminds me to cover my whole body with light before I sleep like he taught me as a little girl.

"Your inner world is just as important as what your eyes and ears perceive in the outer world. You must not lose touch with it, but you can't let it control you either," he says before he kisses me on the forehead. He glances at the book in my hands, "One chapter only, then lights out," he says.

I'm reading a book about King Arthur and the Knights of the Round Table. I want to go on a quest when I grow up.

I dream of a light being wearing a shirt made of many colors of light. He bathes me in emerald light. And he talks to me silently right into my mind.

"I've come to help you heal your toes. We'll use light." He holds up his palms and emerald light flows out of them. "Use your imagination to see the emerald light going into your toes. First see your toes made of light then gradually turning into flesh."

I wonder who he is. I ask him if he is Jesus.

"I'm Hilarion, Master of the Emerald Green Ray of Healing and I've come in answer to your parents' prayers," he said, "and at the request of Sophie."

My mother prayed for me. I'm so happy. Maybe I'm not bad.

I ask Master Hilarion why this happened to my toes. He says I must take care which thoughts I listen to and learn to distinguish which thoughts are mine, which come from the light, and which might be there to harm or control me.

"Every being has a unique gift," he says. "You must protect yourself with an armor of light. Be brave like the Knights of the

Round Table and grow up to share your message. Keep writing in your journal. You are a scribe."

I ask my brother how to spell scribe. He brings me the dictionary. Spelling is hard for me. I mix up all the letters. There is a word for people like me, but I can't remember it.

I wonder about Master Hilarion. Did my dreams make him up because I needed him? Or is he real? I write in my journal. Then I hide it under my mattress.

The swelling in my feet is finally going down after two weeks. They got ridiculously big like clown feet. Now all the skin is peeling off them. Yuck. But underneath they're pink and new. I use my thoughts and feelings of love to call the Green Ray to make new healthy tissue, and day by day I feel less afraid of having them cut off.

It's three weeks since I froze my toes. The doctor announced today that the danger of gangrene has passed. I'm allowed to stand a few minutes at a time. Soon I will be allowed to take a few steps. My parents saved my feet with that massaging. I will be grateful to them for all eternity. How did they know what to do? Parents have a hard job. I understand better why I'm my mother's trial. I caused them a lot of worry and expense because I don't have any common sense.

I'm nearly ready to go back to school. I missed five weeks, nearly lost my toes, and encountered a reptile and a light being.

"Were those beings real or did I dream them?" I ask Anne.

"Dreams *are* real," she answers. She's very sure of herself for a six-year-old.

Winter retreated while I grew new flesh in my toes. Spring is in the air my first day back at school. I feel shy and stupid. Everyone knows what I did, that I froze my own toes. Some kids want to see them. I want to hide in the girl's bathroom.

My best friend, Lynn, tells them, "There's nothing to see!"

Then she takes my arm and walks me away.

The second day back is easier.

I'm happy that it's finally June. My father is reading the morning newspaper. I reach for the Rice Krispies and pour some into my bowl. I listen for the snap, crackle and pop when I add the milk. My father looks up from the paper and says to my mother, "Carl Jung has died."

"Who's that?" I ask my father.

"He's a Swiss psychologist whose ideas I learned about in a psychology class at Columbia."

I want to ask, what ideas? My mother is looking at me. I read her mind. She knows I want to ask about this man, Carl Jung.

But she says, "Don't make so much noise when you eat."

Exercise: Healing

It helps with healing if you can get in touch with the child in you, by which I mean the timeless eternal world of your inner child, a world which isn't bound by too much civilization or too much rationality or education. This is the Self who speaks to you in your dreams at night. Use your imagination to reach out to her. Picture your child-self, the aspect of your being who still believes in magic, who still listens to her instincts and knows that dreams are real. She knows that it is the spark of Divine in you which can heal you. And more importantly, she knows how to access the shuttle to the Divine itself in order to connect your spark with the Creator. You can carefully open your channel to the Divine in two steps without drugs.

Step One:

Imagine a great Central Sun with an infinite capacity to create anything. This Great Central Sun is full of photons. Each photon was created by the vibration of Love. Every photon has all the power of the whole to create and heal. You are made of these photons. Acknowledge yourself as part of this great Light. See yourself and everybody and everything as photons from this Divine Light. Imagine an eternal vibration of Love, an endless fountain of light and love, creating billions of photons, each one a creator. Let this sink in. This is the hardest part.

Step Two:
Imagine yourself in a shuttle made of light. Your shuttle can move right into the heart of this Divine Sun where you can heal yourself of anything because you are part of this Sun even when you are in a human body. This Sun has every color of light. To heal yourself you can choose the Green Ray energy of healing, or Pink Ray energy of love, or Violet Ray energy of transmutation or any color light ray you like. Bask in this light. Know yourself as Divine. See yourself healed.

Chapter 4

Bigfoot on Okinawa

It's 1969. I'm twenty and living on Okinawa for the summer with my husband, Finn, who is in the Air Force. He dropped out of Cornell and signed up. Many guys my age are going to Vietnam. I have nightmares that I'm there in the jungle with them trying to stay alive. I wake up sweaty from these dreams.

Finn wasn't sent to Vietnam. He was sent to language school at the Presidio in Monterey to learn Mandarin and Vietnamese. He almost didn't get top security clearance because he was engaged to me and I have relatives behind the Iron Curtain. I hadn't known about them, but of course, my Grandmother Anastasia immigrated from the Ukraine to the United States in 1917. She escaped through Poland where her boyfriend, who later became my grandfather, father of my father, carried her through the sewers of Warsaw to escape.

I'm alone on Okinawa a lot while Finn flies spy missions over Vietnam. Sometimes his Russian counterparts are flying so close they wave.

Last summer I visited Finn in Monterey where the Air Force was training him not only in languages but also what to do if his plane was shot down. As part of the training he was shut in a coffin for ten hours. I told him I would use mental telepathy to stay in touch with him while he was in the coffin.

After, when they let him out, he told me that at one moment he suddenly thought of a giraffe, another moment he thought of us on the beach at Carmel. I showed him a list of the images I'd sent him. He hugged me.

This summer I'm spending a lot of time alone sitting by the South China Sea. It's turquoise. I breathe in the color. It feels like peace and joy stirred together. A boy in a red loincloth just dove from his canoe into the sea. He's diving for pearls. I get ideas and sometimes hear messages when I sit here silently doing nothing. Today I heard, "You're a Nephilim. Learn to use the power of this connection to the celestial realm."

I don't know what a Nephilim is or if that's even how you spell it. We don't have a dictionary. I wonder where the library is on Okinawa. I'm afraid of this word Nephilim. Unless maybe it's a cousin of Cherubim, and Seraphim. I don't mind hearing that I'm a scribe, and that I must write, but Nephilim sounds strange. The other words I still don't like are gangrene and dyslexia.

I feel I'm supposed to be doing something, that it's time to wake up and do it. Is it writing? Maybe I'm just lazy. I feel a growing tension between my inner world and outer reality. As a child my inner world was far more important and present to me than the outer world of the adults. That's somehow flipped into the opposite with the outer world prevailing now.

In the outer world I'm a college student majoring in English. I don't know how any more to think like a child, freely, without constraint, or how to stay open to that other timeless eternal realm. I think I got married partly to have sex with Finn. We believed all things were possible, even marriage for life at nineteen and twenty-one.

I sit by the sea searching for my own personal myth to live by and wondering what a Nephilim is. I want my inner voice to guide my choices. I also want to know more of the other greater aspects of sex, sex as a form of worship to Eros, to relationship, even as a way to connect to God. I know only the Christian myth which condemns sex outside of marriage as well as sex just for the joy of it.

My mother drilled this into me, so I was a virgin when I married Finn. My mother is a formidable force in the external world. I know nothing of her inner world. She's smart and she has a lot of common sense. Despite her anger at God she lives by the Christian myth which I have never believed in. No real God would say sex is only for procreation. That's a man-made idea. I want to have a personal relationship with the Divine without some man-made religion interfering and messing it up and making me feel shame.

Finn and I live in a stucco house here on Okinawa. We're not alone in it. I don't mean the geckos. I feel the presence of invisible beings. We sleep on a futon on tatami mats. They smell wonderful like grass. I lie in the dark beside Finn and listen to the palm trees rustling overhead outside the windows. I imagine that the tall palms are women wearing floor length silk gowns and long white gloves. I see them gliding across a ballroom in the arms of men in eighteenth century evening dress. This ballroom and these people are so vivid in my imagination that I feel part of me is living in that world too. Usually imagining this scene comforts me but tonight I'm restless. I lie awake for a long time. Finally, I must drift off, because suddenly I'm face to face with a Bigfoot type creature. I'm terrified. What does he want with me? Why is he here? A moment later I am the creature. I am Bigfoot. This creature is me. I am a monster. I don't know if he is in me or I am in him.

I must be screaming because Finn wakes up to find me across the room on all fours.

"You're safe. I'd die for you," he blurts out. Then he turns on the light and sees my face. "But don't ever scare me like that again."

"What did you see?" I ask.

"Come to bed now, it was just a bad dream," he says crossing the room and pulling me close. I'm not sure he believes that. I know, I don't. It was an encounter, as real as any I've ever had. It was no dream. Bigfoot was here in this reality, in our bedroom. He was at the very least someone's actual thought form of Bigfoot. Why was he here? Did I attract him? Was he sent? This wasn't a symbol in a dream.

A symbol is something I create in my dreams and my waking life to show myself how I'm feeling when words aren't adequate to express my meaning. Symbols are a way in which I communicate with myself, while both awake and in dreams. And the symbols can have multiple meanings, like a butterfly for example. If I dream of a butterfly I may be showing myself that I'm transforming, or something in me will be beautiful but short-lived, fleeting, or that I'm about to take flight in some sense, or that the gestation period for something is over and change is coming. When I contemplate the butterfly as it appears in my dream and the way I feel about it, I then understand why it appeared and what it's telling me. The same is true in waking life. If I keep seeing butterflies I wonder about it until my intuition figures out what message they bring.

Each of us has a kind of personal warehouse of symbols peculiar to us which recur in our dreams. Our dreaming self uses these symbols to communicate to our waking self how our inner self is feeling. In my warehouse of symbols there are bears and reptiles, roses and crosses, my grandmother's house, treetops, horses, flowing rivers, flying people, fish, men I don't know in waking life, tidal waves, spaceships, mountains, pyramids, sandy shores, light beings, far off planets, temple goddesses, elephants with jeweled foreheads, but no Bigfoot, ever. He just isn't in my warehouse. Did I pull him in from the collective unconscious, the universal, archetypal warehouse of symbols we all share? No. Bigfoot wasn't a symbol I created in a dream state. He was there.

I've heard of Bigfoot creatures, and know they supposedly live inside the planet and don't come around humans much. They were the bodies provided for souls brought from the planet Maldek when Maldek blew itself up 700,000 years ago. I read once that Bigfoot beings were being kept now in case of nuclear war on Earth as possible bodies for human souls because they would better survive radiation than human bodies can. But who

21

is keeping them? It must be the guardians of this planet who are concerned that Earth's atmosphere will get destroyed in a nuclear war. But why was this Bigfoot here in our bedroom? Was he trying to possess me? It felt like an attack from the dark side, like the time I was eleven and froze my feet. I need protection. I ask Master Hilarion, the angels and God for help.

Today is July 20, 1969. My Bigfoot experience is fading. It's been two weeks. The next night after it happened Finn came home from base with a fellow officer who is a psychiatrist. He asked me about my "dream" of Bigfoot? He was kind. Did Finn think I was cracking up? I have to stop writing in a minute. We don't have a TV so I'm listening to the radio, eating a peanut butter and jelly sandwich waiting for news of Apollo 11. Any moment Neil Armstrong and Buzz Aldrin are going to walk on the moon.

I wish my sister, Anne, was here. I picture all the times she and I saw the moon in out of body experiences as children. I wonder if Neil Armstrong did that too when he was a kid. Travel in spaceships takes a long time to go any distance, light years. Humans are evolving and will be able to travel anywhere in any galaxy instantly like we do in our dreams without a spaceship once we all understand that the universe is One Being. I know children can do this, but adults have forgotten how. I have forgotten how. I dreamt I wrote a story about how some higher dimensional beings are incarnate on Earth to help us. They looked just like us but they still understood their power to create. In my story I called them Wanderers.

There's a typhoon warning. August is typhoon season on Okinawa. Finn and his plane are being evacuated off the island. He came home an hour ago to bring me our old Chevy and have me drive him back to the base. Okinawa is full of old American cars. Ours is a ten-year-old 1959 silver Chevy Impala with big fins and cat's eye taillights. I'm crazy about it. And it has a great radio. My favorite song this summer is "Aquarius." I wish for it to come on the radio every time I start the car. Sometimes the universe obliges me.

"Fill the bathtub with water and keep away from the windows," Finn says as he brushes my lips with a kiss and heads toward his plane. I want to wait and watch him take off, but he says, "No, you better get going home. And stay inside."

The sky looks ominous.

"I'm not sure when I'll be back," he calls over his shoulder.

By the time I get home the wind is already bending the trees so far over that their fronds touch the roof of our house. It feels like nature has collected a lot of pent-up feelings from all of us living here on the South China Sea and she's going to transmute them and release them for us and then we'll all feel better. Maybe this is another way nature helps us, using floods and typhoons and hurricanes and tornadoes as a release when the psychic atmosphere gets too thick.

I park our Chevy next to the house under the large palm tree. The sky is growing dark as I dash through the rain to the front door. I dry off and curl up on the sofa on the far side of the room from the windows to think for a minute. Even though it's only 3:00pm it's so dark that I have to turn on a lamp. The windows are rattling. Stuff is flying around outside, the top to a metal garbage pail, an umbrella, a paper bag. While the bathtub fills I put the water on for tea, thankful for a gas stove in case the power goes out, which reminds me to see if we have any candles. In a kitchen drawer I find a box of ten-inch tapers. Apples will do as candle holders if I core out the centers. I reach for our transistor radio and flip it on while I prepare the apples to be candle holders. "Something" by George Harrison is playing. It's just been released and this is only the second time I've heard it.

A huge crash startles me. The car horn is blaring. I look out the window. The big palm tree, its roots torn out of the ground, is lying across the hood of our Chevy. The sight hurts. Only moments ago the palm was alive, conscious, breathing, waving her worried fronds around with the other palm trees. As I retreat with the radio to the bedroom on the other side of the house from the car horn I wonder how long a car horn can blow before it stops. It's like the Chevy is yelling, "Get the palm tree off me, she's crushing me." Something hits the outside of the bedroom wall. It feels heavier than a flying garbage pail lid. Then blackout. The bedroom lamp goes out. I head back to the kitchen to light the candles and return to the bedroom with them.

I look over my summer reading list from college: *Lady Chatterley's Lover, The Tropic of Cancer, To Kill a Mockingbird, The Prime of Miss Jean Brodie, A House for Mr. Biswas, The Golden Notebook, A Clockwork Orange, Herzog, In Cold Blood, Portnoy's Complaint, A Single Man, The Autobiography of Malcolm X*. I choose *Lady Chatterley's Lover* and escape into her world. Only for a moment do I think of Bigfoot.

I open my eyes. It's light out and quiet. The horn has blown itself out. There's no wind or rain, only silence. The house is still standing around me. I open the front door and walk outside. There's a new lightness as if the storm has cleansed the atmosphere. That must be why I loved storms so as a child. They relieve tension, bring things back into harmony.

I walk over to the palm tree lying across the hood of our Chevy. I kiss her goodbye. Later Finn calls from base to say he's back and can I pick him up. I ask him to hold on while I see if I can push the palm tree off the hood. It's too heavy.

Today is August 30th. I have a letter from my sister in my hand and I'm leaning against the kitchen counter reading it, enjoying deciphering her straight up and down and somehow loopy handwriting all crowded together on the page, as if she's saving space to cram in all the words. I love this handwriting and would recognize it anywhere. I lift the page to my nose and sniff it in case there is some lingering scent of her. She writes that two weeks ago she and her friends went to the Woodstock Music Festival.

"Richie Havens sang a song called 'Freedom.' He looked like he was channeling it on the spot," she says. "That's how magical the festival was. People were channeling and giving readings, sharing food and shelter, and tripping out in a good way, despite the mud and rain. Somehow even the rain was right. No one minded it. We were all one."

I read and reread her letter.

In two days I will fly back to the U.S. for college. I won't see Finn again until he next gets a longish leave, maybe Christmas time. We're sad to part but we don't talk about it. We make love.

Exercise: Using the Liminal Space between Waking and Sleeping

When you're lying in the dark, drifting off to sleep, slowing down, turning inward, try to feel your brain waves shift into Theta. Observe the images that float before your mind's eye in this liminal state between sleeping and waking. On this border you can shift your consciousness to focus on various neighboring realities. You can use your consciousness like it's a movie camera. Choose one of the images floating before your mind's eye and follow it. Let it show you something or someplace. You may be visiting another life in which part of your greater Self, your Over Soul, is living. Notice what symbols your unconscious chooses. Ask yourself why your unconscious chose this particular symbol or setting.

Chapter 5

Angel on My Window Seat

It's the summer of 1974. Last night Nixon resigned as President of the United States. I watched on TV with friends at their apartment. Nixon's underbelly, his greed for power and need to look good, are right out there on display for everyone to see. How does he bear the shame? How can he face his wife, his daughters, the TV cameras?

I'm twenty-six and I have my own shame. Finn and I have been divorced for three years. It feels bad to write that. I broke my commitment. My mother was furious when I wanted to marry Finn at age nineteen before graduating from college. She said I was too young to know what I wanted to do with my life or how much commitment and loyalty a life-long partnership requires.

"You don't realize what you're committing to," she said. "Take your head out of the clouds. Marriage isn't as simple as you think."

She was right, as she usually is about how to best get on in the outer world. I wonder if she is ever bothered by another voice, a timeless eternal figure inside her that has a different view of things. Is it just me, her child with no common sense, who feels the pull of two selves, an outer "do the right steps in life" person, and an inner being who exists outside time, in the eternal world and dreams that all things are possible, even a personal relationship with God?

I hurt Finn, who I love. I blush with shame writing this. I force myself to stay with the feeling in the hope the blush is the fire of karma burning. Would it have been more fortunate had I been less willful or been prevented from getting what I believed at nineteen to be my heart's desire? Often it turns out in life that this is the case, although we kick and scream at the time when our will is thwarted. But even my powerful mother stops short of interfering too forcefully with the free will of another adult, even of my free will, since I turned eighteen.

Now I must bear my guilt for hurting Finn. I must look directly at what I've done, see how I wounded him, and acknowledge that part of me which inflicts pain on others. If I don't, I'll never be able to breathe freely. I see that it was my hubris, my belief that, at nineteen, I could know what I wanted for my whole life. I realized too late that I didn't know. I didn't know who I was myself. I still don't. With no sexual experience beyond making out at parties I didn't know what sex was either, how intense and symbolic a union it is. Too late I saw what I really needed was a relationship with myself and freedom to grow out from under my parents' wings and do things like go to Woodstock with my sister, not follow Finn halfway around the world to sit by the South China Sea alone. But full of myself when I'd insisted on marrying him, I'd said to my mother, "Love conquers all."

"Don't be absurd," she said.

In a way my dark side, my shadow, is the easiest part of myself to see. Most of us can see our selfishness and greed, our envy, our pleasure seeking at another's expense. We've all heard the word ego. But the ego is just the smallest part of myself which I wish to know. I want to know hidden things. How do my own light and shadow make a whole? There is a light in each of us, our very own spark of the Divine. But where is my spark, covered with tarnish and hidden in the hem of my skirt?

I want to find it again and polish it. I imagine this spark is a key which opens a secret door to the channel which we all have that takes us right upward through the dimensions to the Divine. It's the channel that psychics and healers use to bring down information. It's the same channel Edgar Cayce used to contact the Akashic Records.

Despite my guilt and shame I'm moving on. I'm in a new relationship. We live in Greenwich Village. His name is Andrew. I met him in Sanford Meisner's acting class. He's a singer-songwriter under contract to Warner Brothers. Each morning he sits down to write as soon as we return from our favorite breakfast spot, a little hole in the wall on West Fourth Street. He's disciplined and dedicated to his art, busy fanning his creative spark. He's in the grip of his daimon, his creative spirit. I admire him for it.

Our apartment has two working fireplaces. One in the living room and one in the bedroom. How did we get so lucky? The whole time we were looking I kept focusing my attention and imaging what we wanted, over and over, and we got it. Getting in the right mind set and asking for something to manifest works. But you must be in the Tao, as the Chinese call it, for this to work. I wonder, is the Tao the same thing as the unified field? I think so. Joy puts me in the Tao, opens my channel to the Divine. Joy creates magic when you couple it with your heartfelt intention. When I'm joyful it's as if even the objects around me change, become brighter, more vivid and lively, and the room looks different; it even appears to change shape. I see each single wildflower in the bouquet as an individual with its own purpose.

But when I ignore my inner voice, my channel closes and sometimes a glass, a plate, a vase, slips out of my hands and breaks on the floor or even breaks right in my hands to let me know I'm shut down and out of sync, out of the Tao. This no longer surprises me. It's my unconscious at work, trying to let me know I'm disconnected, out of balance, ignoring something which wants to become conscious. I ask myself what it is that I'm refusing to look at. What have I been ignoring that made me drop the glass or bump my head or take a tumble or get gripped by a mood? If I don't face whatever it is I'm avoiding, the next accident will be bigger and the next even bigger until I wake up and get back in balance.

The buzzer for the front door is ringing. It must be the piano delivery and I want to watch the men hoist it up to the second floor and through the front windows. Andrew's uncle died and left him his concert grand piano. A few weeks ago we went uptown to New York Presbyterian Hospital to visit him and found his body lying in his hospital bed without his Soul. Andrew went to tell the nurse his uncle was dead. I stayed with his body. Uninhabited, it looked completely different from a body enlivened with a spark of the Divine, an actual sliver of God energy. We really are God, and without God's spark enlivening us, our bodies are like a lump of clay, albeit a lovely lump of clay which does us a great service. This is not to say that clay isn't conscious, because everything is conscious in its way, even a hammer and nails.

The piano is safely inside now, its legs restored to its body, and Andrew is busy getting to know it. I'm lying on the sofa reading *Seth Speaks* by Jane Roberts. I occasionally glance across the room at this large shiny black new arrival. I admire its curves, feel its presence, try to discern its consciousness. It is a being. I will make friends with it, appreciate it, maybe love it. Andrew will no doubt love it. It is made of stars just as we are, only its atoms are put together in a different way from ours. I wonder, is the piano conscious of us? Two answers bump into each other in my head. One speaking in my mother's voice says, "Don't be ridiculous." The other says, "Yes, the atoms in the piano are alive and conscious and even conscious in their way of you appreciating them."

Seth explains that the same atoms constellate everything. He also says the same thing about time that physicists tell us. Linear time is an illusion particular to the Third Dimension. He means it's only relevant here in the Third Dimension, but not in other dimensions. Only here do we have a past, present and future. At a deeper reality everything is happening at once. We just accept the convention of time so that our heads don't explode by perceiving too much at one time. Our human senses are not designed to perceive everything happening at once. Our human bodies focus on this specific Earth world to such an extent that we're nearly hypnotized by it. We don't see all the other realities and time periods intermixed with it, overlaying it and weaving through it.

Another mind-blowing thing is, how can there be past lives if there's no past? According to Seth our multidimensional Self is living all our lives simultaneously even if we perceive some of those other selves living lives in different centuries. Our perception is an illusion, a camouflage. We're made of many selves, like a diamond with multiple facets, and we sometimes visit our other selves in our dreams. Some of our lives are even in other galaxies. I have dreamt of myself on other planets. Within our physical body there are subtle layers that represent other physical existences which our Over Soul is simultaneously living. These other lives are connected electromagnetically to the atomic structure of our current body. By current I mean, the body we identify as ours now in this life.

As I read Seth all this sounds vaguely familiar to me. I feel that I know it from somewhere. Still, it shakes and rattles my twenty-six-year-old human self. It's a lot for her to absorb. But my other Self, my inner Self, feels very excited by these ideas.

When I feel frightened or destabilized by an idea, I remind myself that the most important thing is to live my life in this time and space in the Third Dimension, to stay grounded here. That's what I came to Earth for, what each of us came for. Our human life is what gives our eternal Self the opportunity to live a third dimensional existence.

Another thing Seth says which amazes me is that we're actually creating our reality with our minds, even our physical reality. He explains that we continually use our subconscious minds to create not only our own bodies but also the world we perceive. And that world is not constant. We blink in and out of our world even as we're creating it, but we ignore the blinks in order to experience our reality as continuous. During the blinks we're in a different reality with different root assumptions and governed by different laws and with different types of material and nonmaterial beings. We could attend to the blinks if we chose to, but what we saw might shock us, so we mostly block them out.

Seth describes how while doing the dishes one evening Jane Roberts looked out her kitchen window and observed a different reality in which she saw a creature make itself out of rain. Jane Roberts is the voice channel for Seth. A window remains open in her psyche which allows her to perceive multidimensional reality. She survived the usual closure that happens after childhood. She has no fear of being a voice channel. My outer self is afraid of being a voice channel. Like most people I receive information in the dream state and as intuitions, and through my inner voice.

Sometimes when I'm doing a mindless task like washing the dishes I space out and go somewhere else. Then if Andrew comes up behind me and hugs me, I'm startled and jump out of my skin. I think many people have this experience.

Now he warns me first, "Ground control to Susan."

Reading Seth helps me understand some of the things I've experienced all my life. It makes me wonder how many different realities and different dimensions there are. Seth says humans are having a unique experience in the Third Dimension because most beings moving through the Third Dimension in other galaxies don't get to have a physical body. Instead they are oscillating consciousness without material form. According to Seth humans are very fortunate to have this opportunity to experience a physical body.

Maybe it's because of reading Seth so much but I've started dreaming in a way I haven't dreamt since childhood. I find myself outside at night flying over treetops, and when I swoop down lower, I can read the signs. Last night I flew over a town called Ronkonkoma. I've never been there while awake. I don't even know if it's a real place but I have a strong urge to find out. I mostly stay above the treetops in these dreams because it's so beautiful to see all the green leaves swaying in the breeze. Last night wasn't a normal flying dream. It felt too real to be a dream at all. I'm sure I was there above the trees. I've read about yogis who do astral projection, which Jane Roberts calls "projection of consciousness." Maybe I'm doing it and that's how I get above the treetops.

Tonight Andrew and I are hanging out at home celebrating two years together.

"We are so lucky," I say to him, "we humans here on Earth. We have these beautiful material vehicles with our five external senses but we also have our internal intuitive senses."

"Bring your external ears over here for a moment," he says. "I want to play you Randy Newman's new album."

We lie on the floor side by side to listen. We hold hands. It feels good to hold hands with another human. For a moment I am somewhere else, maybe in a cathedral or a big church. I see Andrew from behind standing at the altar with a girl who has long dark hair. I know it isn't me because I have blonde hair. Then the vision is gone and I know we will not marry. He will marry this dark-haired girl. My heart breaks a little. I force myself back to the present moment.

We listen to Randy Newman's distinctive voice. We both love "Marie." He squeezes my hand. In the song Randy Newman tells Marie, "I loved you the first time I saw you, you looked like a princess the night we met, with your hair piled up high I will never forget."

"Love at first sight," I say to Andrew.

He nods. "Sometimes it's like that. You just know."

"How does that work? Why this person and not that person? There's no thinking involved. It's a kind of magic."

"Love is the great mystery," he says. "I falter before the task of writing a song to even attempt to express it."

We lie there in silence listening to Randy Newman sing his thoughts and feelings into our consciousness.

The album ends. "Want to hear it again?" he asks.

"I do."

Whatever happens in the future, for this moment we are together and I want to be here now. We lie still, fall into silence again and get lost in Randy Newman's voice. When I listen to music I enjoy, I move into a different state of consciousness. It's close to my normal waking consciousness, a neighbor of it. I even hold my head in a different way when I'm in this other neighboring consciousness and my breathing changes. I see this happening to Andrew too.

The album finished, Andrew says, "Come to bed."

He puts the LP back in its album cover. I see he's still transported by the music.

"Randy Newman has a great sense of humor," I say.

"My father used to quote Schopenhauer," Andrew says. "'A sense of humor is the only really Divine quality of man.'"

I think about that. Laughter can feel Divine like when mirth bubbles up from your heart and you surrender your self-consciousness and allow the joy to overtake you. Andrew's father must have understood this.

He died last year, suddenly, of a heart attack in the back seat of the car while his driver was bringing him into the city for a meeting about his idea for lasers. He was born in Hungary and came here as young scientist to work at Los Alamos. He invented the LP because he didn't like the way 78s interrupted a symphony. He also invented the 45. How did he get those ideas? Did he have a foot in the timeless world? So where is he now? Maybe inventing more stuff in another dimension.

I wonder where all my 45s from the 1960s are. I had a case for them which I used to carry to parties in junior high. It's weird to think that if there's no time and everything is happening in the now, then junior high is happening right now too.

"Come to bed," Andrew says again.

In the middle of the night I wake up. There is an angel standing on or maybe floating just above the window seat, emanating soft golden light. I'm frightened. Then inside my head I hear, "Fear acts as a distorting lens, a barrier, focus on your heart to dispel your fear."

Is this angel communicating with me through mental telepathy? I relax and breathe in the sublime energy. The angel continues.

"It's time to begin writing. Consciousness can be turned in many directions. Turn your consciousness inward toward the formless realm. You have many friends there waiting to communicate with you. Write down the messages you receive in story form. Use your gifts. Fulfill your agreement and be the scribe you're meant to be. You are never alone. Help is always at hand. Learn to call on it."

The room goes dark. I feel bereft. Have I blinked into another dimension or did the angel visit mine? I wake Andrew.

"You're dreaming," he says kissing my forehead.

I know it wasn't a dream. An angel was here in our room in this dimension. And there's that word again, scribe.

Seth teaches that no system of reality is closed. Our thoughts and actions enter other worlds and other world happenings enter our system of reality. We believe our thoughts are secret and harmless, but Seth explains that not only do other humans perceive our thoughts, but our thoughts appear in other realities as objects, alive and vital where they are used as the raw material for creativity in any one of an infinite number of ways. Similarly, the thoughts of other beings drift into our reality. Did Andrew's father pick up the idea for the LP and the 45 from someone else's thought in a different reality? For that matter did Einstein pick up the idea for the Theory of Relativity from someone's thought in a different reality? And where did the idea for the atomic bomb come from? The atomic bomb is made of the same atoms as we are. I wonder how those atoms feel being used to make a bomb.

I prop myself up in bed, light a candle and reach for my journal and pen. I replay the angel's message in my head and write it down.

Andrew and I are lying on the grass in Central Park. We just took Acid, aka LSD. I'm staring up into the trees, looking at the individual leaves. I see each leaf as a dab of paint on a canvas.

"Andrew, I think the impressionists were on something like Acid when they painted. I can see what they saw."

He's not listening. Tears are running down his face and I follow his gaze to an elderly man in a wheelchair.

"Yes. Growing old and weak can be sad, but it's better than dying young," I whisper to him.

He laughs. I wipe his tears with my sleeve.

The sun is setting. It's many hours since we took Acid this morning and we're hungry. We leave the park and head to the Carnegie Deli. We're happy to get a booth. Next to us there's a table of four old ladies with white hair. They're all wearing black dresses and black shoes that tie. One of them is saying something to the other three.

"She's lying," I say to Andrew.

"How do you know that?" he asks me.

"Look at her Pinocchio nose growing longer and longer as she talks. Don't you see it? It's a foot long sticking out straight from the middle of her face."

"Eat your sandwich," he says. "It's time for this trip to end."

Last week we went to the TM center and each of us in our own private ceremony received our mantra. We've been meditating together twice a day for twenty minutes, morning and evening. A few times our friends Jimmy and Maggie have come by and the four of us have meditated together. They're the ones who introduced us to TM. They trained as TM teachers in London before they came to New York. I'm hoping this meditation practice will help me build the discipline and structure to become a scribe. I'll ask the angel if he comes again.

Today I'm on my way to Sheridan Square where I have a dance rehearsal at the Greek Art Theater, a lovely little underground amphitheater. My thoughts are running before me like a babbling brook as I walk the short distance. I say to myself, "What am I waiting for? I'm supposed to be a scribe, but I don't know how to begin. How will I get the information?"

On the way home from rehearsal I buy a copy of *The Village Voice*. There's an ad, inviting writers, artists, healers, astrologists, musicians, actors to come to the Algonquin Hotel to learn about a new community. The ad is signed only, Zhenya. I shiver when I read the name. I feel like someone has walked over my grave.

I walk into our apartment and see Andrew sitting on the piano bench. He has a pencil in his mouth and his fingers are on the keys. I feel such love for him. He looks up and smiles and turns back to his work. I go into our bedroom and sink into the armchair next to our bed to think.

I look at *The Village Voice* ad again. Is this ad a sign to point me in a direction where I can find a way to begin fulfilling my agreement to be a scribe, to bring in information from other realms and write it down? I suspect I can't be a scribe until I'm in harmony with my inner self, with the world of my unconscious, because it is that world which opens to other realms. It's the archetypal world of the unconscious which connects us to the Divine. This connection to the Divine gives meaning and dignity to our human life. Our ego-self on the other hand organizes our life in the outer world, finds us a place to live, keeps us from accidentally stepping into traffic, stuff like that. These two selves are partners. Conscious and unconscious, inner world and outer world, Godself and ego-self—it's a lot for us humans to hold at once. We are complicated beings with a lot going on.

I put down *The Voice* and sit a while longer without moving.

"Follow your own destiny. Don't get in the way of Andrew's. Stop allowing yourself to be distracted. The meditation is good, deepen your practice. It will help you fulfill your mission."

Who said that? I look around for the angel. I don't see anyone.

I go to the Algonquin at the appointed time. I meet Zhenya.

Exercise: Feel the Angelic Presence around You

Many of us go through life unaware of intervention from the angelic realm. We don't realize the help they provide when we're in need, often even before we ask. Hindsight will show it to you if you look back at times in your life when you narrowly averted disaster. Maybe you were about to step into the bike lane unaware of the approaching motorcycle and you suddenly became aware of what you were doing or maybe you felt an invisible hand pull you back out of harm's way. Maybe you were about to make a bad business deal and seemingly by accident something came to light to warn you just in time. Maybe you met just the right person at the right time in your life to bring something to light. Or maybe a thought popped into your head that solved a problem.

Comb through your memory looking at your life events and try to see where those in the angelic realm intervened to help you. Thank them. Ask them to keep watching over you. Maybe start to keep a record of these interventions from the angelic realm.

Chapter 6

The Berkeley Psychic Institute

I'm twenty-nine and living in Berkeley, California, with Zhenya. We're renting a big two-story house on Oakley Street a block south of College Avenue. For most of the world it's 1979, but in Berkeley it still feels like the 1960s.

We have a deck. Really, it's the flat roof of our double garage, but it's heavenly, thick with vegetation including the overhanging branches of a lemon tree and several lush loquat bushes. Zhenya sits out there smoking pot, listening to the Stones' *Exile on Main St*, reading *Zen and the Art of Motorcycle Maintenance*, all the while dreaming up new schemes for changing the world. To help support us he's writing for several magazines including a new one called *Omni*. I'm working as a waitress at The Trident overlooking the San Francisco Bay. At work as I serve the customers I listen to the restaurant's playlist. It includes a lot of Earth, Wind & Fire and the Bee Gees. When there aren't many customers I stand and watch white sailboats fly by carried on the wind over the bay. My mind lifts me up out over the water above their sails. I fly above them in the translucent light over the bay.

This afternoon I'm off work and sitting out on our own deck under the branches of the lemon tree reading *One Hundred Years of Solitude*. Zhenya comes out and drops two letters in my lap. My mother writes to tell me that waitressing isn't a good use of a college education. She still hasn't forgiven me for the divorce, or for marrying Finn in the first place for that matter.

I open my sister's letter and let out a whoop. Anne's pregnant! I want to do a jig. Zhenya doesn't hear me because he's trying out this new thing he bought to send to his teenage son. It's called a Walkman. Sony has just released it and it costs two hundred dollars. That's more than the cost of two hundred gallons of gas. Gas is eighty-six cents a gallon.

I think about my sister. This will be her second child. She already has a two-year-old daughter, Eloise. She says she feels guilty like she'll be replacing Eloise. When she holds Eloise and reads her a story, she thinks to her herself, "How can I do this to her?"

I will write and remind her that later Eloise will be glad of a sister or brother as I am glad of her. She'll see.

Zhenya and I met in New York at the Algonquin Hotel where he was interviewing people to create a community to share skills and knowledge. He named it Apple Skills Exchange. Apple offered monthlong, affordable classes in everything from The Game of Go, Jungian Dream Analysis, Meditation, and Moped Maintenance, to, Waking Tours of Soho, Playwriting, Photography, Reiki and Thai Cooking. And Apple did become a thriving community. It was big fun and brought thousands of New Yorkers together both in our Fifth Avenue loft and in the living rooms, kitchens and studios of artists, healers and teachers all over the city.

Apple is where I met my first Jungian analyst and learned that Jung also felt the presence of another inside himself, and the tension between this inner timeless being and his outer self which had to navigate the world. As a child Jung called them his number one and number two personalities. Much later when he was a psychiatrist, he called them the Self and the ego. It was a big relief to me to realize Jung knew that each of us is both a temporal and an eternal being, and that I'm not weird. As children we are mostly our inner eternal Self. We don't yet have a persona or much of an ego. By adulthood most of us have developed a persona and we've learned to use it to interface with society.

Jung held on to consciousness of his eternal Self all his life. He understood that at the center of every individual there is a light, and in that light our two selves are united in harmony. He dreamt of this inner light as a shimmering island with a flowering tree at its center. Reading Jung makes me feel less of an outsider in life. Jung's point of view makes the old ache from my mother's attitude toward me hurt less. She does understand better than I how essential it is to adapt to the outer world. It was she who warned me as a child not to blurt out to people what I saw that was going to happen to them.

"Everyone has free will, whatever you think you see about their future," she said. "Nothing is set in stone. Keep your visions to yourself."

She was right about that. We do all have free will. And there are many probable futures which could manifest. Psychics generally see the most likely one.

But back to Apple Skills Exchange. Apple even had a farm upstate for weekend classes. The one time my father visited the farm he said, "Susan. What are you doing here with Zhenya? He's like the king of a banana republic. Why not live your own dream?"

I sagged in the knees when he said that.

For a couple of years Apple was a shared dream which brought together thousands of New Yorkers. Then, without telling anyone the whole story about him, Zhenya hired a comptroller called Al. About three months after Al started working for Apple I woke up in the middle of the night from a dream about him. In the dream I saw Al stealing away on a donkey, loaded down with saddle bags full of coins. I felt Zhenya lying beside me in the dark, awake. I told him my dream.

He responded, "I have to tell you something, but not here."

I struggled to get out of our waterbed which was by this time springing tiny leaks courtesy of Zhenya's cat, Alfie. A few minutes later we'd crossed the street and were sitting under the 4:00am fluorescent lights in Dunkin' Donuts. Folding back the lid of his paper coffee cup to take a sip, Zhenya began.

"I kept something from you, from everyone at Apple."

"Go on," I said.

"Al had just been released from Rikers when I hired him. He was serving time for embezzlement. I haven't been able to reach him on the phone for the past two days."

"Does he have Apple's checkbook?" I ask.

"Yes, but he needs two signatures."

On a visit to the bank later that morning we discover that Al had emptied Apple's bank account the previous day by forging Zhenya's signature.

When we return to the Apple loft to tell the others, the first question is, "Everything?"

"Everything, all the money we had to pay the teachers and ourselves and keep Apple afloat," Zhenya says, "and Al's disappeared."

Before he became a hippie, Zhenya was a savvy Madison Avenue advertising guy who invented the slogan "The Pepsi Generation." Even if hiring Al was self-sabotage because he was tired of Apple and wanted to move on to his next big idea, I wasn't pissed off at him for it, though many in our community were both angry and sad. Zhenya gave us Apple then he took it away. I rationalized that taking a risk and giving someone a second chance were more valuable personal qualities than savvy. Besides I was guilty of the same hubris myself. When Zhenya first introduced me to Al I'd shivered because I had a momentary vision of him behind bars and I said nothing until my dream of him stealing away on the donkey with the money bags.

I wouldn't describe Zhenya as a Svengali, though some people at Apple did. It is true that whatever he touched came alive. And sex with him was like connecting into the hard drive of the universe. It was more than the physical pleasure. Sex is bigger than two people making love. The ecstasy of orgasm is both real and symbolic as two become one. Orgasm is our

Creator's gift to us, a little taste of Divine Oneness to show us the state in which the universe eternally dwells. The Hindus call it Ananda, bliss.

A psychic who was part of Apple early on told me, "Don't miss out on this relationship. It's going to be some fantastic roller coaster ride."

But another of our resident psychics warned me. "Zhenya's a mind fuck. Don't let him get his hooks in you. He'll lift you up to heaven and drag you down into hell."

Were they seeing the same thing and interpreting it differently? They felt free to speak of what they saw, of their visions, in a way that I don't. Because there's always some interpretation involved in relaying a message to another person and even to yourself, we need to approach visions with care.

After we turned out the lights and closed the door on Apple, we loaded up Zhenya's Volkswagen bus, and along with two cats and a dog, drove across the country over the plains and through the desert to arrive in California, Berkeley to be exact. We've been here nine months. Despite the loquats and lemons and sailboats flying across the bay, I miss New York.

It's a soft summer evening. I'm watering the white roses along the side of our house. Donovan, Zhenya's wolfhound, is lying by me. Through the open window I hear Meat Loaf playing on the record player, "Two Out of Three Ain't Bad." Zhenya loves Meat Loaf's energy. Last summer at Apple Farm it was Rod Stewart whom he played constantly, especially, "Tonight's the Night." He gets captured by certain songs that give him a dopamine rush.

I stand still holding the hose, growing more and more intoxicated with the gentle fragrance of the roses as I watch the water sink softly into the ground seeking their thirsty roots. The setting sun is shining through the water as it emerges from the hose. I can't take my eyes off it. I'm mesmerized. Then without knowing how I'm somewhere else. I'm outside a large stately old stone mansion. Standing before the mansion is a carriage pulled by two horses. A man in dress from the eighteen-hundreds steps out of the carriage. I know him. My heart pounds. His face is very dear to me. He turns and offers his hand to a woman in the carriage. Their eyes meet and hold one another. My heart races. The woman is me. I'm wearing a long dress, a bonnet tied loosely under my chin and short gloves. I'm holding a small drawstring purse. It is my eyes which are looking into his.

Zhenya calls to me through the window, startling me. I jump and the hose sprays the side of the house and Donovan who leaps up.

"Are you planning to drown those roses?" Zhenya says.

Where I have just been feels more alive to me than right here in Berkeley. I want to go back but it's gone, the opening between the worlds is closed. I know I've been in that world before. I recognize it from my dreams.

And it's not the only other reality I visit in my dreams, and — what do I call these experiences? Daydreams. Trances. Shifts in my brain wave frequency. Blinks into simultaneous lives I'm also living. Some of the places I travel to are in what looks like the past on Earth, some in what looks like the future somewhere else. Seth says it's just as easy to "remember" the future as it is to remember the past. At times I feel I'm existing in the center of many probable realities and which reality I experience is just a matter of where I direct my attention, my consciousness, almost like it's a movie camera. Am I directing it or is it being pulled somewhere? These other realities are so compelling and so real, just as real as what I think of as this life I'm living. Why shouldn't they be just as real, when what we think of as real isn't real either if Seth is right. Seth says it's all a camouflage we create together below the level of our conscious awareness.

Jung purposefully directed his consciousness using a technique he called active imagination. Active, because he consciously chose which image to follow and then concentrated on that one image, not allowing other scenes to draw him away from that one. He would drop down into the unconscious to the land of the Self to visit these inner realities and meet the beings there, like Philemon, who became Jung's inner spiritual guide to the unconscious, his guru. Jung discovered he could speak to Philemon and to all the inner figures he encountered and ask them questions and find out why they had appeared to him. It was Philemon, Jung said, who showed him the absolute reality of the inner world. I want to speak to these two beings emerging from the carriage and ask them why they appeared to me.

I'm seeing a Jungian analyst here in Berkeley. At our next session I will ask about these blinks where I feel as if I'm in a different reality. Am I accidentally doing active imagination and wandering around in the inner world? I want to learn to do it intentionally, carefully, to keep a firm hold on my outer life, my conscious self, and not get swamped by the inner world. I wonder if there are an infinite number of other realities, and how and why they suddenly appear. Am I unconsciously stumbling into them? I know I'm not doing it consciously, as Jung did.

The tapestry of our existence, of our whole Self, is perhaps too complex for our third dimensional self to comprehend. Maybe only our greater Self can be aware of all our existences. What I've observed about my visits to my other lives is that they happen when the psychic atmospheres of the two existences are in rapport. Then a bleed-through of realities occurs and a door opens between two lives that otherwise seem separate.

"Come on," Zhenya says handing me a helmet and turning off the hose. "We're going for a spin through the Berkeley Hills."

I climb onto the motorcycle behind him and wrap my arms around his waist. Despite the present joy of gliding through the lush hills in the soft evening light, the other reality I just glimpsed and my feeling for the people stepping from the carriage stay with me. At this moment my consciousness feels malleable, like a camera lens I can turn from one reality to another. Maybe every reality is created by the person observing it. With no observer are there just floating atoms or molecules or photons waiting to be transformed into matter by an observer?

One nice thing about being on the back of a motorcycle is that you can think your own thoughts. The arrangement isn't set up for conversation. As we speed along in silence through the twilight, I review the other scene and focus on the man offering his hand to help me from the carriage. Is there a reason I saw this very scene this evening? Maybe he was holding out his hand to somehow help me in the present. Maybe I am meant to understand something, learn something from it. This woman could be another probable self, another manifestation of my identity. I have such warm feelings for them.

It's a hot afternoon. I'm on Telegraph Avenue doing errands. I spot a flyer for the Berkeley Psychic Institute in the window of a bookstore and realize that it's just around the corner. I walk up to what is a large cream-colored three-story house with a wraparound porch. I go in and make an appointment for a reading for the following week. When I get home I don't mention this to Zhenya. This omission is part of my shadow, my underbelly, as my therapist calls it. I'm being withholding and dishonest. Why? What is it I fear?

Today's the day for my appointment. A young guy at the desk shows me to a room upstairs. I sit in a chair facing a woman who looks like she's in her late thirties. She's wearing jeans, a tie-dyed T-shirt and sandals. Her long reddish-brown hair flows down her back. She welcomes me. I've had many readings in my twenty-nine years on this planet but for some reason I'm uncharacteristically nervous today.

Beginning with my root chakra she tells me how open each chakra was at birth and how open it is now and what is affecting it. After a few minutes she stops this process to inform me there is a cord attached to my third chakra, my solar plexus. The cord, she says, is attached to an outside entity who is draining my energy. A big rocking motion makes us both look up toward the ceiling then down at the floor.

"Is the house shaking?" I ask her.

Almost immediately the door opens and two other psychics come in, an older man and woman. They also sit down across from me. The three of them concentrate to stabilize the building. Pretty soon the house stops rocking and shaking. The man explains that the being who placed this cord in me is here in energetic form and he's trying to disrupt the session and distract us by shaking the house in order to prevent me from removing the cord. The older woman explains further.

"The being who placed the cord is not originally from our galaxy. Just as there are spectrums of light, there are spectrums of matter. Our system of physical reality here on Earth in the Third Dimension is on a place in the spectrum of matter which is not particularly dense. The being who placed this cord is from a different density. He's very powerful, but his power is stuck which weakens him. Because his power is stuck you are more powerful, but you aren't stepping into your power. You don't receive your power because you fear it. It takes great discipline to welcome, to hold, and to employ our gifts so they will bear fruit. I see you standing on a mountaintop holding lightning in your hand. You have let go of your power, forgotten how to wield it. You must learn to hold your power, otherwise you will be continually vulnerable to attack. And you will fail to fulfill your mission. Discipline yourself. Discipline sharpens the spear. Discipline is also the shield that keeps you from being infiltrated by negativity."

I look across at the three of them with gratitude and wonder how I am to get over my fear of power. How I am to sharpen my spear and make my shield.

"The being who placed this cord is misusing his inner senses. He no longer remembers that it is the mind which creates matter by using intention to propel thoughts, feelings and desires into form. He is aware that you can help him remember many things, but he is trying to do this the wrong way by siphoning your knowledge and energy. You have an old agreement with him, a note tucked into a pocket in your psyche so to speak, a kind of destiny point. This agreement made in another life will have to be dissolved for us to remove the cord and restore your energy."

The younger woman tells me to follow the cord with my inner vision from my third chakra to find the being attached to it.

I close my eyes and affirm my connection to my Higher Self and to the Divine. Using my breath I travel inward and ask my Higher Self to show me what I need to know. A vision forms before my inner eye. Bipedal human-like beings, but taller and with longer necks and smaller heads are moving toward a bell-shaped spaceship. I am among those walking toward the entrance of the ship. I stop and turn to have a last look at someone who is not permitted to come. It is Zhenya. The scene is as transparent as water.

"It is my partner who placed the cord," I tell them.

The older woman asks my human self for permission to dissolve the agreement and remove the cord. I agree.

"Before we can remove it you must also request the permission of your Higher Self, who made this agreement," she says.

I make the request. This granted, they proceed using the power of their thought and intention supported by my and their own Higher Selves, our guides and The Divine. The dissolution is quickly accomplished.

When it is over the older woman tells me to look in the mirror. Before I leave, as if she has read in my mind my concern about how to discipline myself, she explains, "Self-acceptance and discipline are two wings of a bird. Self-acceptance is the state. Discipline is the action. Without discipline you are constantly at the whim of your mind. Discipline your mind in order to hold your state."

For the past few days since my healing at the Berkeley Psychic Institute I feel lighter, freer. I know the action I must take is to leave Zhenya. I need a plan. Where will I go? I pick up the telephone and call information for the number of the admissions department of The New School for Social Research in New York City.

Today my application to graduate school arrived in the mail.

We're sitting on the deck drinking gin and tonic under the lemon tree when Zhenya looks at me and asks, "Are you really doing this?"

A month flies by and it's time for me to leave Berkeley. On the day, I water all the plants and flowers and trees on the deck, and say goodbye and thank you to them. I know we have to leave for the airport in a few minutes, but I can't rush.

At my gate Zhenya thrusts a fat manila envelope into my hand. "For you to read on your way to JFK."

I'm the last one to board. I walk backward onto the ramp leading to the plane door, unable to turn away from him as he holds me with his eyes.

I buckle my seatbelt and look down at the eight by ten envelope in my lap. Zhenya is a writer so this is going to hurt. I open it and a loquat from our deck with its leaf still attached falls out, small and orange, calculated to prick my heart. Then I see the photos. There's one of the inside of our refrigerator, one of our rumpled white sheets in the morning sun, a bunch of others. At the bottom is a white rose from our yard. The plane hasn't yet taken off and I haven't even read his words or looked at all the photos and the tears are already coming. I start to read the two typed pages.

"Susan, I can't do it gently... You've been all gifts, the rooms you created, the dinners, the hanging plants and garden flowers. You introduced me to order and touching the things of my life more lightly—coming into a room, your voice on the phone, your body on the bed next to mine, your hair like butter, the scent of your bath soap on your skin, these are the gifts I always understand and, in my own churlish way, acknowledge. You introduced me to love *ein-sof*, love without end. But now come the Deacon Blue days soon to be played out in a hollow ringing place called today without you. You are depriving me of you. And Susan, I'm scared shitless."

I can't read any more. I can't face this right now and I stuff the pages back in the envelope.

"Suffering is always the beginning of the healing," a voice inside reminds me. "Grasp your sword and shield. And when the green light comes on and the aircraft door slides back, take a deep breath and jump feet first."

Exercise: Open Your Inner Senses

It helps to open our inner senses, our inner knowing and intuition, if we can turn off our external senses. That's why deprivation tanks were so popular in the seventies. A cool quiet room, a soft surface to lie on, an eye mask and ear plugs can help you turn off your external senses, but they aren't necessary. Lie down and bring your focus to your body. Notice any place where you are holding tension. Caress those places with your breath until the contraction releases. Imagine your breath untying all the knots with its magic.

Next shift your attention to your third eye. See it spinning open to reveal a scene. Don't control the scene. Don't judge it. Just follow it and let it go where it wants while you observe it. Wonder a little why your third eye is revealing this scene in particular. What does it want you to know, to see about yourself?

When you feel you've gotten the message the scene is offering you, write it down in your journal. Describe what you saw and how you feel about it, what it might mean.

Chapter 7

Shape Shifting

I found these little things called Post-Its in the bookstore. The cashier said they were just created this year, by accident. It's 1980 and this is my first week of graduate school. Thank God, my student loan came through. I have an interest rate of 9%. That's supposed to be good in this financial climate and the repayment won't start until I graduate. Between the loan and my waitress job at Windows on the World at the top of the World Trade Center I'll be fine.

In the larger world, Ronald Reagan is running for president to replace Jimmy Carter. I'm for Jimmy Carter. I admire his way of being. I like that he put solar panels on the White House roof.

I'm sitting in the lobby of an apartment building on Fourteenth Street writing in my journal and waiting for my old friends, Maggie and Jimmy, to arrive in their U-Haul. I'm here to help them unload and move into their new apartment. A guy with a Mohawk haircut is speaking to the doorman. He's walking toward me. He sits on the sofa across from my chair.

"I'm Robin," he says.

At that moment Maggie comes into the lobby and we both get up. "Oh good, you've met," she says. "Jimmy's outside with the van."

It turns out that Jimmy's the guitar player in Robin's band. The four of us carry their records and books, chairs and tables and mattress and guitars into the elevator and down the hall to their new apartment. I like Robin's face. I think about him a few times over the next couple of weeks. I wonder what his story is.

I'm meeting Maggie tonight at The Bottom Line to hear Robin's band, Buskin and Batteau. "They're great," I whisper to Maggie between songs.

Even though it's late when I get home after the show the phone is ringing as I come in the door. Zhenya tells me, "You're off the hook, kid. I've met someone."

I hang the phone up on the kitchen wall and sink down on my knees on the kitchen floor and thank God. It's only at this moment that I realize I've been afraid these last few weeks that Zhenya would fly in from California and come after me. I'm free. He has a new woman who wears the face of the goddess for him.

I started therapy with a new Jungian analyst. He's more intense than the one I saw in Berkeley. He likes to focus on my mother, especially my dreams about her.

John Lennon and Yoko Ono just released a new album, *Double Fantasy*. Not since "Imagine" have I been so moved by a record. He must have wandered here from a higher dimension to be singing about "how the world could live as One." I play *Double Fantasy* constantly.

Robin and I started dating. Tonight we're uptown. We leave the band shell in Central Park and enter Lincoln Center from the Central Park side to stand by the fountain. It's all lit up. We're watching the water shoot up toward the night sky with the giant Chagalls behind it in the glass opera house when two police cars and an ambulance careen by, sirens blaring. I shiver. The moment splits. We head back downtown, and Robin drops me off at my apartment.

I'm getting ready for bed when the phone rings. It's Robin. I'm surprised because I've only just said good night to him.

"John Lennon is dead. He was shot. The sirens we heard... He and Yoko were arriving home from the recording studio, just walking into the courtyard of their building..."

The dark lords, I think to myself.

"Susan? Are you there?" Robin asks.

"I'm here."

The sky is falling. How can Yoko bear it? Christmas comes and goes in a hush.

I'm waiting for Robin and David, and Maggie and Jimmy to arrive and help me move my stuff. It's four months since I met Robin and two months since John Lennon was murdered. Robin and I are moving in together. It's Valentine's Day. I'm in love with him. I admire him. Robin's studio is in the same neighborhood in the Village where I used to live with Andrew before I moved to California. There's my buzzer. Someone's here.

After a week I feel settled in. Robin is easy about stuff. I have to leave for work in a minute for my waitress job at Windows on the World. It's a good gig except for the elevator ride to the top. There are fifteen miles of elevator shafts in the two towers. The elevator I take to the top is the size of a room and holds about fifty people at a time. It bangs against first one side then the other side of the shaft as it ascends. The energy gives me goosebumps. Maybe I'll look for a different waitress job where my feet are on the ground.

I tell my therapist I have nightmares about the towers falling down. She asks if I feel my life is always being blown apart by some powerful force within me, like the tower card in the Tarot. I ask her how you can tell if a dream is about yourself personally or about something outside of you, something in the greater world. She says often you can't. Sometimes you just have to wait and see. I'm up in the top of the tower now and changed into my uniform. It's a tailored beige dress with pale pink piping around the collar and cuffs, sheer stockings and beige kitten heels. I'm waiting for lunch service to begin and looking out of the huge windows right into the sky. Fluffy white clouds float close by. I can see most of Manhattan and all the bridges which cross the East River into Brooklyn and Queens.

Robin cut off his Mohawk and is letting his hair grow in. His partner David is still pissed off about the Mohawk. He says that Mohawk cost them a record deal. We're watching M*A*S*H reruns on TV tonight and drinking tea and sharing a pack of little sugar donuts. The show just ended. I close my journal and run a bubble bath. Robin sits beside the bath to talk to me. Our kitten Dwight comes in and balances on the side of the tub.

With Robin I'm learning more about sex. It was different with Zhenya. He used to come and take me the way a man takes a woman by catching her up, making her feel his desire for her, stirring her desire to meet his, his passion igniting hers. And I would receive him, his otherness, his masculine energy. And he would know my welcome, feel our opposites combining to create our own alchemy. But I felt in the deepest recesses of myself a small holding back, a shrinking back from him, a little hiding for fear.

It's different with Robin. He also comes to me like a man, but I have no fear of him. There are moments of stillness as we lie together, before I unfold. I don't want to hide anything. I don't want to carry Eve's shame. Ever since she bit into that apple it's too easy for women to regard ourselves as bad, fallen, seductresses, secondary, our nakedness and desire for sex as sinful, as only lust rather than a Divine union. These attitudes lurk in our unconscious. I don't want this to be part of my relationship with Robin.

He looks into my eyes and whispers, "I've never held anybody the way I hold you. Be my window. I'll be your door."

Waves of desire crash over us washing us clean of the past, clean of Eve's legacy. Sex is both baptism and confirmation. I want to be consumed in him, in a Divine conflagration. No longer a separate being, I find myself again, as part of a new whole with him. In this alchemical consummation we travel out into the universe as a Oneness.

After, when we return to our separate selves, I notice Robin looking at my eyes in a strange staring way. But I feel so peaceful I fall asleep before I can ask him about it.

The next evening I return from school to find Robin singing a song into his hand-held tape recorder. He says, "It's called 'The Girl with the Golden Eyes.'"

"Oh?"

"When we make love your eyes change. They turn golden."

"A little shape shifting?" I say, wondering about it.

This isn't something I feel comfortable sharing in therapy. I'm still afraid of being seen as weird which is ridiculous since my therapist is a Jungian and Jung actually held conversations with his inner beings and believed they were as real as people in the outer world.

Instead, I consult an intuitive I know on Morton Street. She tells me that when we make love I appear to Robin in the body I had on Atlantis. "Among other subtle changes your eyes become more oval and turn golden."

This doesn't surprise me.

"You had a life there together," she says. "A lot of beings from Atlantis are now incarnate on Earth for the changes that are coming."

I tell Robin that our life on Atlantis bleeds through to this reality when we make love because the psychic atmosphere between the two existences comes into rapport, into resonance. He smiles but doesn't comment.

My favorite class is Jungian Psychology. I gobble up Jung's ideas. Ever since first working with a Jungian analyst during Apple I've been fascinated by Jung.

According to the analyst I saw in Berkeley, what I've been accidentally slipping into all my life, is a similar thing to Jung's process of active imagination. My new therapist agrees but emphasizes it's important to be intentional and to focus on only one scene at a time. I wonder how much she believes that active imagination is our consciousness shifting to actual real inner realities in which our greater Self is living?

When Jung dropped down into his unconscious he described in detail his encounters with other aspects of his greater Self. Meeting Jung through his writing feels like knowing him. He speaks right into both my heart and my mind. And what he writes about dreams opening into vast unconscious worlds and affording us the freedom to visit these worlds, helps my understanding of consciousness in as profound a way as Seth does. It's easy to float off into starry fields musing about all Jung's ideas. Fortunately my waitress job keeps me somewhat grounded, despite my feet being 1,362 feet off the ground when I'm at work at the top of the tower. We have to know these facts in case one of the guests asks.

It's 1982. Robin and I are still living in his studio apartment along with his violin, mandolin, guitars, baby grand piano and my record player, albums and books, and our two cats, Ernie and Dwight. Each of these beloved beings has its own personality and radiates its own energy. All together we make a big group.

I'm working on a paper about Jung's two selves when I smell fresh sawdust. I put down my pen and look around. Nothing. It's the smell I remember from when I was a little girl and my father was sawing wood in our garage to build shelves. I remember saying hello to the nails and the boards. Did someone, an angel, a guide, drop this scent and this memory into my mind just now to remind me that I always knew this, about the consciousness of all things?

Yesterday I was reading Barbara Hannah's book on Jung. She was his good friend. She said that Jung recognized and acknowledged the consciousness of objects. When staying in his tower he would talk to the pots and pans. Before he began using them to cook he would apologize for his absence from the tower and ask them for their cooperation while he prepared a meal.

Friends of Robin's got a new thing called a CD player. CDs are so small compared to albums and they don't get scratches as easily. They play us a Billy Joel CD. Robin says it sounds different from vinyl. I wonder if these little discs will replace albums. I love album covers. *Thriller* is lying on a nearby chair. I glance at the album cover and feel the images affecting me, Michael Jackson's white suit, the way he's holding his hand, the expression on his face, his signature on the cover.

When we get home Robin puts on the album *Arc of a Diver* by Steve Winwood. We listen together. Life is always changing. Phone answering machines, Sony Walkman, Post-Its, CDs, computers and floppy discs, VCRs. A few people even have phones disconnected from the wall which they take with them when they leave home. They call them their cell phones.

"Don't hold on too tight," I hear in the space around my head. "Let things unfold. Welcome even things you don't want, welcome especially the things you don't want."

What things? I wonder.

A lot of thoughts drop in that don't originate with me. They feel like someone else's thoughts. Some are startling, like revelations. They seem to arrive unattended, but they must be sent by guides, angels or my Higher Self, unless I'm just stumbling on them.

Jung's inner guide, Philemon, told him that thoughts are like animals in the forest. They just are. You come upon them. You don't create them. You tune into them. A thought crossed my path yesterday as I was walking along Bleecker Street. I heard it inside, not with my external ears. "Your subconscious mind is creating this reality which you are walking through. It's not real, it's all a camouflage."

Whose thought is this that I happened upon?

Robin's beginning to write jingles now as well as songs. It comes easily to him. He comes up with things like "the unsinkable Cheerios" and "Heartbeat of America, today's Chevrolet."

I received my master's degree in psychology in May and am beginning my PhD this fall. My friend Carrie asked me how I will marry psychology with my other ideas, the mystical ones?

"Jung didn't see the conflict," I tell her. "He believed in a vast timeless inner world, guided by far different principles from outer reality. But he never wanted to be called a mystic. It was all part of psychology for him."

"Yes," she said, "Jung was brave and willing to pay the price for being different. And he hated it when Freud called him a mystic."

The weather changed. It's autumn. Classes started last week. My favorite class is dream interpretation even though the professor smokes during class. He sits cross legged on top of his desk facing us and lights up one Marlboro after another. Sometimes he lights the wrong end.

In my dreams I'm often in a different life and doing a completely different job from here. In some dreams I use color, light and sound to heal. I often dream I'm a scribe in what looks like the Middle Ages. The study where I write in these dreams is ancient, familiar and beloved. I believe we meet our greater Self, our eternal timeless Self, in our dreams. I don't share this in class. I don't have Jung's courage.

I do share all my beliefs with my therapist now. In the Jungian world I feel accepted and understood. Outside of it, especially by intellectuals who distain a belief in God or anything greater than man, and there are a lot of them at The New School, I feel judged for my beliefs and my feeling side. I feel inferior, not as smart as they are.

I know it would be healthier to accept my feelings of inferiority, to welcome them, but instead I try to rationalize about what's wrong with intellectuals who insist only on rationality. I tell myself that excessive rationality can rob one of vitality and that intellectuals often neglect their feeling side as well as the primitive aspects of their personalities. They sacrifice these aspects and force them to go underground which can make them one-sided. When the truth is, I envy them. I wish I was an intellectual, even a scholar, a Faust. But I don't have it in me.

And worse, I'm more like Mephistopheles than Faust. My shadow, the dark side of my being, with all its sinister aspects, like jealousy of people smarter than me, is still very alive in me. Robin is smarter than me and better educated. At least I'm not jealous of him. I like that about him.

Despite the shame I feel for hurtful things I've done to other people, like saying mean things, being willful, insisting on being right, my ego mind is still busy rationalizing my behavior. I'd like a major demolition of my defenses so I can see the truth about myself and stop keeping secrets from myself, secrets that fester in the dark. I want to say, who cares what the ego is up to. It's always the same nonsense. God help me.

It's the week before Christmas and my sister Anne is visiting with her two little daughters. We're walking up Sixth Avenue in the falling snow when we suddenly decide to take a taxi up to Rockefeller Center to see the tree. I step into the street and hold out my arm. A yellow cab pulls up to us. Anne, I and her little daughters climb into the back seat. The youngest, age three, is on her lap.

"What are we doing in this man's car?" she asks her mother.

Her question delights Anne and me. For a moment we can almost remember how to think like a child ourselves. As a three-year-old growing up in the country, she has no idea what a taxi is. She has no schema in her mind for it. She asks how we've suddenly come to be in a stranger's car. Jung talks about the world of the child and how free it is. He calls it the "timeless world," the world of our eternal Self, and he contrasts it to adult life which belongs to the world of time. We each must find a way to balance our eternal timeless Self and our temporal self who must navigate this life in the world of time and space.

Artists seem to me to do this most easily. They still play. Robin plays. I fantasize about having a studio to write and play in, a separate place different from where my adult self is living. The studio would be the home of my eternal Self, who isn't really of this world, but who carries a different perspective on things, the part of me that sees from the mountaintop, rather than the valley. This is what Jung's tower was for him, the home of his eternal, timeless Self.

Spring is in the air. I'm walking by The Village Cigar Store on Sheridan Square and I hear a voice in the ether around me say, "You and Robin will part. Your time together is coming to an end."

I stop walking and stand still. No. We're happy. I love him. I'm not doing it. This time I will be constant. I decide the message must be the dark side in me making trouble. But it didn't feel like that if I'm honest, it felt like a neutral fact. Maybe it has some other meaning. Months go by and we are fine. I try to forget that message. It creeps back in. Why can I never stay put and build something and be loyal and committed? I can never get too comfortable in a relationship, too complacent. Things can suddenly take a right turn. I do it to myself. Why?

An inner voice answers me. "At a certain point you wall yourself off because you fear being vulnerable. Instead you could try to bear the fear. That is the true strength."

My mother has said this to me too, in her way. She's accused me of repeatedly blowing up the landscape of my life, never building anything lasting, never really trusting anyone fully.

My sister Anne suggests I consult an astrologer to see what looking at myself through the lens of the planets and stars can add to my understanding of why I always seem to upend my life.

"Didn't Jung have an astrologer?" she asks.

"He did, and he also consulted the I Ching and the tarot."

My friend Maggie tells me about an astrologer that John and Yoko consulted. I make an appointment and two weeks later walk down to Soho to meet the astrologer.

"You're a Uranus woman," he informs me. "Uranus doesn't do marriage well. Uranus women don't sit home nursing babies. Theirs is a multidimensional reality. The universe is their partner. Once anything becomes conventional, you're out of there."

Hearing this is painful. I don't want to be unconventional. I want to be steadfast and loyal to someone. But deep inside I know I must live what I am.

The astrologer elaborates, "The Venus in you longs for love and relationship but your Pluto's not having it. He'll force the death of every relationship one way or another and throw you out into the street, allowing only the universe to be your bridegroom."

I don't like hearing this even though it gives me cover from taking responsibility.

He continues. "Venus is the beauty in you and Pluto your blood and guts. Your Venus hates your Pluto. It's too vulgar for her, too brash, too dark, too underworld, always lurking in the shadows making trouble. But the Scorpio in you loves the Pluto because it plunges you into the underworld. Pluto incites, digs up, provokes, exposes. This combination of Pluto and Venus is what makes your writing so powerful."

"I'm not a writer," I tell him.

"You should be," he answers. "With all the Uranus in your chart you're pulling in information from other realms. You may as well write it down and share it. Pluto will provide the texture. But you'll have to be on your game, do your real work, be who you incarnated to be, or Pluto will eat you for breakfast."

This isn't the first time I've been told my task is to write, to channel from the formless realm and anchor the information in the Third Dimension.

"Pluto strips away illusions," he explains. "It shows the beauty in the darkness and exposes the mystery in the shadows. Pluto keeps it real, keeps you from being seduced by appearances."

I start to thank him, and he adds, "Pluto loves science fiction. Try putting the information you receive in story form and Pluto will be less likely to pull the rug out from under you."

"I don't even read science fiction," I begin, but he interrupts me.

"Let romantic love be a source of adventure, fun and discovery, but keep it loosey-goosey and focus rather on being a scribe."

I thank him and leave in a kind of trance. I walk down the street thinking about what he said about keeping romantic relationships loosey-goosey. This explanation feels like a giant cop-out to excuse all my breakups. Love isn't loosey-goosey for me. Love is how I experience my Soul.

Jung pointed out that it is only in relation to a living partner that we meet our own unconscious, our greater Self. A man first finds his Soul, his anima, in the face of a living, breathing woman, like Dante did with Beatrice. The same is true for a woman. She first sees her Soul, her animus, in the face of a flesh and blood man. We are not aware that we have projected our inner being onto this person who fascinates us. We're not aware that what we see in the other person is a mirror of our own inner opposite, our own contra-sexual self. The inner woman in a man, his anima, and the inner man in a woman, her animus, are real beings which we first encounter as unconscious projections onto another person who captivates us, even bewitches us. This other reflects our Soul to us.

My relationships with men are what first made me conscious of who my inner man is, of what he is like. My inner masculine at this moment wears Robin's face but standing behind him are the faces of all the men I have loved, my grandfather, my father, my brothers, Jung, each of my partners. It is my love for these men which provides the hidden passageway, the doorway, between my inner self and my outer-self in the world. Our Souls become whole in the presence of the other, and the inner opposite which he represents in the physical. It is the inner union as well as a physical union which gives life to the Soul. It is love for another which connects our inner and outer worlds.

Love seems to me to be a subject for the gods, a paradox and a mystery, a blessed divine mystery which is out of our human hands. It never feels like a choice to love someone. Before you know it you're caught in it, possessed by it.

"You're captured," Jung said of love in an interview near the end of his life, "it's not no choice."

And yet there is truth to my mother's words that I am at fault, that I destroy everything with lack of commitment. I do it, not the planets. I have free will and I make choices. I create my destiny.

As to the astrologer's other insights, they felt right. I've been told before I am meant to be a scribe, that that is my destiny, my work in this dimension, my reason for incarnating. Instead, I'm getting a degree in psychology. Hopefully when I have something to say I will write. Jung was both a therapist and a writer. He was judged for his beliefs but he remained steadfast and true to himself. Being true to his own discoveries cost him his relationship with Freud and the whole Vienna set. For a time this made him feel like he was going crazy, but he persevered through the fear and pain and ostracism.

Instead of returning home after the astrologer I'm walking over to the Hudson River. I wish my father was walking with me. When I felt bad as a child he would remind me that it's OK to be a little different, that it's important to be oneself, to live what you are.

Jung says that too. "If you're a sausage, don't dress yourself up like a pheasant."

I'm standing at the river's edge as if I am waiting for something. Watching the light play on the surface of the water I remember my father telling me once when I was little and in trouble with my mother, "It's that you think with your heart. She thinks with her head, which is the usual way with adults."

But maybe I need more adult thinking to accept responsibility for my actions, in order to become a loyal and committed person. I want to face my fear and replace it with a will of steel. I don't like who I am. I want to be steadfast and loyal to one partner always. So far I am failing. But then again, does it count, is it fulfilling, to be steadfast only to one's purpose rather than to a partner? Can the inner self be partner enough? I hope so.

Staring at the river I feel calm, and my focus shifts inward. I let go a bit, breathe into my heart, accept that there are questions which I can't yet answer. I feel myself drop down further inside myself, away from my outer senses. I reach for that other wiser, less judgemental, part of me who uses a different set of senses — her inner senses — which see with a different view than regular external human senses which fasten our focus in the outer world. I feel a peace wash over me. Maybe all my failures are a necessary part of the journey, and so far I can only see part of the story. In this moment standing at the edge of the river I do know that my waking self is only a fragment of who I am and that my outer life rests on my relationship with my inner being. She knows that all life's disturbances, all life's questions and failures are illusions. Disturbances exist only in what the Hindus call the outer world of Maya. The inner world is the true reality. I want to hold onto this perspective or at least keep rediscovering it.

Walking home I stop at the corner for a red light and look down at the curb. Someone has stenciled on the sidewalk, "This isn't real."

Exercise: Consultation with Your Soul

Lie quietly, breathe gently, little sips of air through your nose and into your heart. Savor your breath for a few moments. Acknowledge your inner being, feel her presence within your heart. Your inner being is the aspect of you which has the widest perspective, the eternal view from the top of the mountain. Your conscious self has a less far reaching more temporal view, the view from the valley.

Ask your inner being, "What do you want for my life that I'm not aware of? Where do I step next?"

The answer may come immediately in a telepathic communication, or it may appear written in the air in front of you or even behind your closed eyelids. Your answer may not arrive right away, but later in the day painted on the side of a building or as something you overhear in an elevator conversation, or as a sign on a passing truck. Watch for it until you receive it. When you receive it take the time to contemplate its meaning for your life. Be patient with yourself. This is not an hour's work.

Chapter 8

Garden Gnomes and Fairies

I'm listening to President Reagan give a speech in Berlin. "Mr. Gorbachev, tear down this wall." He delivered the line like the actor he is, so it was effective. It reminds me of listening to Kennedy's "Ich Bin Ein Berliner" speech with my father when I was a girl.

I live on Bleecker Street, near Grove, with Ali. We met in the library two summers ago while studying for our Comprehensive PhD Exams in Psychology. He's Persian.

The phone is ringing so I turn down the radio. It's my mother.

"Why haven't you brought Ali to meet us? Is he Black?"

"No. You're thinking of Muhammed Ali? You've seen *Lawrence of Arabia*. Picture Omar Sharif instead."

Persians aren't Arabs, they're Indo-European, but I don't explain this to my mother, because for that matter, Omar Sharif isn't Arab either. He's Egyptian.

I woke this morning feeling strange. I feel like I've been very far away in some other world, some other galaxy even. I open my eyes and look around. I recognize the lamp on the bedside table and a small glass paperweight etched with the outline of all the countries on Earth. I know the man sleeping beside me, but not his name or my own. I try to recall who I am in this dimension and can't, but it feels OK not to know. I must have been in a deeply protected area of sleep, on the threshold of other layers of reality with experiences out of all context to this time and place. That's why I'm having trouble reorienting. It happens sometimes. I close my eyes again to try and remember where I've just been. I see myself on a barren planet. A guide dressed in a long white robe is showing me that all life on the planet has been destroyed by nuclear war. At least the planet itself wasn't blown apart. He tells me that this must be prevented from happening on Earth. Why am I being shown this? How can I prevent a nuclear war? I open my eyes. The scene is gone. I turn my head and see the title of the book on my nightstand. *Two Essays on Analytical Psychology* by C.G. Jung.

The man beside me wakes up, turns over and looks at me.

"What's my name in this dimension?" I ask him.

"Susan Plunket," he says. Then as he so often does, he teases. "By the way, we're on planet Earth in the year 1987."

Ali is rarely fazed by my way of being in the world. He's a very grounded human and funny too. He still carries the flavor of the Middle East about him and an appreciation for things unseen, maybe because he was born and raised in Teheran in an ancient culture where it wasn't uncommon in his childhood home for a blind soothsayer to be consulted or for his family and their servants to perform Zoroastrian purification rituals.

Ali changes the subject. "Do you still want to see *Fatal Attraction* tonight?"

I nod. We're both doing our internships. I want to learn Reiki to send healing energy to my patients while I listen to them. With Reiki Two you send the symbols without physically touching the person. I convince Ali to take the training with me. During his initiation he feels his hands grow to one meter each as he sees himself in imagination dancing in circles with a Black man in a yellow kaftan, his arms open above his head. He's never seen this man in physical reality, but he feels like a teacher or guide that Ali knows well. During my initiation I travel to a realm where Egyptians from ancient times are instructing novices in healing arts. Afterwards, when we share our experiences, the Reiki Master explains that the gift of Reiki is presented in a unique way to each initiate.

I've also begun attending a weekly three-hour meditation group where a disincarnate being called Mongka works with us through a voice channel, Pamela. Ali is curious about Mongka.

He asks me if sessions with Mongka are like the séances Jung used to attend in Basel during his student days. "Not really," I say. "Mongka just comes through Pamela when we reach a meditative state that can sync up with his vibration. He focuses mainly on demolishing the ego and purifying the mind through meditation."

Life is good. Ali is good. I trust in his goodness, his fairness and honesty and integrity. I am blessed. We're both writing our dissertations.

The next couple of years I must have been focused on starting a practice because I see that I haven't written in this journal since we graduated, got married and began working.

Ali has a hospital job. I'm in private practice. It's 1991. We just got our first ever computer. We're leaving Bleecker Street and moving to Eleventh Street between Fifth and Sixth Avenues. The best part is that we're going to have a garden!

"Turn up the sound," Ali says, as we pack our records and books. We're listening to the Beatles' album, *Rubber Soul*. Hearing it takes me back to 1965 and my home during my teenage years. I see the album cover sitting on the record player in the bedroom I share with my sister Anne. I see our dresser and our twin beds with their tall pineapple bedposts, my desk overlooking the hillside. Anne played that album over and over. God, she loved it.

Our new garden has been long neglected and needs lots of love. Among other things it's full of empty vodka bottles. We haul away ten big black garbage bags. Together we build a garden table with wood from the lumber store. I devote myself to the garden. I'm in heaven. Things long hidden underground begin to awaken and sprout. I add more plants, peonies, lilies, roses, hydrangeas, and in the shady corner, ivy. I find one very special lily called a Resurrection Lily which will bloom in August. I dig and plant and play music for the flowers, trees and plants. Today we all listened to Bach's *Goldberg Variations*.

Satisfied with my day's work I rinse my fingernails with the hose to get the dirt out from under them like I used to do with my father.

Ali makes a Persian dish of pomegranates, walnuts, and a pheasant, which he shot this morning on Long Island. We gobble it up and stretch out with our books. Unlike me he's always reading psychology. Except for Jung, I prefer literary works. I'm holding *Black Lamb and Grey Falcon* but I can't keep my eyes open. After working all day in the garden I feel the best kind of tired.

I wake up. It's dark. Ali is asleep and the whole brownstone is quiet. I'm standing at the bedroom window looking into the garden. I'm face to face with a small girl of maybe four or five. Is she part of me, part of my Over Soul? Only the screen in the window separates us. There is something strange about her. Her eyes are very large. She motions to me to look deeper into the garden. Two gnomes peek out from behind a peony bush and smile at me. Two more show themselves beside the hydrangeas. They're about a foot tall. The fairies are even smaller and nearly transparent as they land on the roses and lilies. The beings of the elemental world have allowed me the privilege of seeing into their realm. I can barely believe my eyes. I haven't visited this realm since I was a child alone with Sophie or my father in our garden. I pinch myself. Have I ever felt this happy on Earth, this honored? I float through the next several days thinking of them, waiting to see them again.

Ali works full time at a hospital in the Bronx. I have an office down the street from our house. This morning, like I do every Wednesday morning, I went to the Upper West Side for a three-hour meditation and teaching from Mongka, the being who speaks through Pamela. His words bring tears to my eyes. They roll down my cheeks. His way of speaking to us penetrates our hearts making our eyes overflow.

Today he talked about *love*, comparing it to the experience of *feeling loved*.

"Where do you feel loved? Where do you feel love? Is it the same? Everyone loves to be loved. Everyone goes where she feels loved. Have you ever felt love? Have you ever felt the love that wells up from the depths of your own heart? Have you ever drowned in this love? Have you ever abandoned yourself totally in the sea of Divine love in your own heart, or have you merely been content to wander this way and that distractedly looking again for the experience of being loved by another person? Then once this dissipates you feel abandoned. Why not go for love, dear ones? Why not give up fishing for these other species of experience and target your own heart? Why not allow the scenery to blur as you rush headlong into the ocean of love in your very own heart."

It takes days for me to metabolize Mongka's words and to admit to myself that I have gone this way and that way looking for the experience of being loved.

There are usually five or six of us in the group; sometimes Mongka gives each of us personal instructions. Today he told me to consciously allow the Divine to work through me while I am with patients. Sometimes while I'm sitting with a patient, insights come into my head that I didn't have myself. They're just suddenly there, as if dropped from heaven. I ask Mongka if he ever had that experience when he was a human.

He responds simply, "I've never been a human, my dear."

I'm surprised. Then I realize how self-centered it is of me to assume everyone must have been human at some point.

My father has been ill. Mongka tells me that my father will recover and will remain on Earth for years yet, but if I want, when the hour of his transition arrives Mongka will be with him.

"The prayer of a child for a parent is always heard," he says.

It's Wednesday again. It feels like just a second ago it was last Wednesday.

Mongka announces, "Your daughter is coming soon."

Ali and I are in the process of adopting a baby from an adoption agency in San Antonio, Texas. They told us it could take a year. It has only been three months.

"She's very bright," Mongka continues. "She'll need that to deal with you, my dear, to deal with your belief that you're always right. Do you see it? Do you see how it keeps you from experiencing the Divine? You overestimate what can be accomplished by being right."

I do see it. I've become my mother, always thinking I'm right, that I know best. It makes me cry seeing that I'm so invested in being right at the expense of being loving. The tears feel good, honest.

Mongka gives me a moment then says, "Make friends with your humiliation. Accept it. Feel the feeling and be done. The stillness, the steadiness to stay with the feeling, dissolves it. Accepting humiliation is very freeing."

Then he moves on, "You and your daughter know each other well as Souls. You've been together in many lifetimes. Even now she is your older sister in another life."

When I stand and leave Pamela's apartment my feet barely touch the pavement. I walk all the way home to the Village, Mongka's words echoing in my ears, "Your daughter is coming soon."

We will have a daughter, a blessing beyond imagination.

A few weeks later the adoption agency in San Antonio calls. Our daughter is born. It's May 21, 1994 and there are twenty-one pink roses blooming on the rose arch in our garden. I thank the fairies and gnomes for the twenty-one roses. This is their work. Naturally the elemental beings knew before we did that she was coming to Earth on the twenty-first.

Ali and I return from San Antonio with Charlotte and I carry her to the garden and hold her up to see her roses. My sister Anne arrives to help us learn how to take care of her. Our friends come with flowers and mobiles and car seats and strollers. Ali is making Persian chicken kabobs marinated in saffron, lemon and rose oil, enough for everybody. I am thanking God every moment for Charlotte and Ali. I don't feel weird or lonely. I feel part of the human world. At last.

Exercise: Open Your Inner Channel

Lie down or sit comfortably. Breathe softly through your nose. Let your breath lead you like a gentle hand into your own heart. Close your eyes. Say hello to your spirit, say hello to your guides even if you don't know who they are yet, and say hello to the Divine. When you look inward, when you meditate you are laying the pipes through which grace will flow.

Imagine there is a light filled channel running up from your root chakra between your hips, all the way up your spine to your crown and out the top of your head connecting you to your guides and to the Divine. Think of something or someone you love. Feel your love for them. Love creates light. Pour this love as if from a golden pitcher into your channel and watch it grow brighter. It is your love which opens this pathway and allows you to channel information from higher realms. Daily attention to your inner central channel strengthens it.

Chapter 9

Terror in the Night

Charlotte is two. She can talk but she still communicates with me mostly via mental telepathy. Last year when she was one we moved to a wonderful big apartment on Fifth Avenue where Charlotte has her own room. We get lots of light and face both Ninth Street and Fifth Avenue. Washington Square Park is right down the street. When we said goodbye to the garden, and to the flowers and plants and trees, I wondered, who will love them now, who will love our gnomes and fairies. Will they even visit the garden anymore? I miss them every day. Sometimes I imagine I'm back in the garden visiting with them.

I hug this one tree in Washington Square Park every morning because I am drawn to it. I asked the tree her name and she answered right into the center of my being, "Thea." Theadora means messenger of God. Charlotte toddles over and hugs Thea too.

In the outer world it's 1996. Bill Clinton is president. Gorbachev was pushed out, and Boris Yeltsin is in charge in Russia. My world is Charlotte, Ali and my patients.

In the middle of the night Charlotte wakes up screaming, terrified. The sound of this cry is so bloodcurdling that both Ali and I run to her. She sends me a mental image of a dark being in her room. I tell Ali. For some reason Ali dashes to the kitchen and gets a broom then opens Charlotte's bedroom window. How does he know to do this? From growing up in Teheran? I ask Charlotte where the dark being is now. Telepathically she tells me it's on top of my head. I ask Ali to knock it off my head with the broom and push it out the window. Afterward, he turns the broom upside down and stands it in the corner of the room. "As a protection," he says. We take Charlotte into our bed and put her between us.

The next morning I call a Feng Shui person to cleanse the whole house of any entities. I explain that Charlotte is of Mayan descent and possibly in a Shamanic line. Perhaps some entity in that bloodline is dark and has designs on her body.

Ali got promoted to chief psychologist at the hospital and began teaching at The New School. He works all the time and travels to present at conferences. He's making a name for himself in the world of psychology testing, especially with the Rorschach. He flies all over the world to consult on difficult cases. This week he's in Europe, in Berlin. He's restless. I tell him he has nothing to prove, he's good enough, hardworking enough and smart enough. I wish Charlotte and I had more of him.

Mongka tells me rather than being dissatisfied with my husband to look at myself and see that I am also restless, that my restlessness is a form of dissatisfaction, and that I might focus on my own shortcomings. He says, "It is not your duty to love your husband, it is your pleasure. It is ultimate denial not to be pleased by him." Mongka is right.

I have a recurring dream.

I'm sitting at a writing table in a Medieval study, holding a quill and writing on parchment. I can't read the words but sense I'm writing a history of Earth.

I remind myself that recurring dreams are repeated attempts by the unconscious to communicate something important. I understand that I'm supposed to be writing. But writing what? I ask for the gift of another dream to guide me. On the third night of asking, I have a dream.

I see a light being, a master of some sort, place a chrysalis in the area of my heart, in what looks and feels like ancient times. The being telepathically communicates that the chrysalis holds information and that it will open at the right time for me to transmit it by inscribing it on paper. I will see the words written in the air in front of me and I will write them down and ground them in the Third Dimension.

The dream stays with me for days, it agitates like a burr under the saddle. I discuss it with my therapist who urges me to start writing. I also consult an intuitive in Minnesota, Cyndi, via telephone to ask her about the chrysalis and what my dharma is in this life.

Right off the bat Cyndi says: "It's five below zero here in Minnesota and I'm so hot I feel like I'm on fire. They're telling me you are here to write. You will be given information to bring into the Third Dimension."

"Who's telling you," I ask. "Your guides or mine?"

"The angelic beings around you, your guides, and beings from the elemental world, the fairy realm, elves, gnomes. They all want to help. You'll receive information both while you're asleep and when you sit with the intention of allowing the knowledge to flow through you. Write in the morning. I see you surrounded by light beings seeking your ear. You will have to sort through the many voices. They've been waiting for you to take up your pen. They're showing me a picture of you writing in a beautiful book, filling up the blank pages. It looks like a mandala of gold on the hard cover of the book."

Instead of being pleased about this I feel resistance to this task build up in me. I feel defensive and fearful.

Mongka has told me more than once, "When it's hard for you to do what you know will make you happy, you have reached your willfulness. It's a brittle defense against your fear of your own power, my dear."

Don't be a willful ass, I say myself. You came to Earth, to wake up and to write. Cyndi continues. "They're showing me another scene. You're being taken by a star being to a charred planet, an ash world, an earlier Earth, one destroyed by nuclear war. You fall on your knees at the sight of it and ask, 'Why are you showing me this?'"

This scene of the charred planet feels familiar to me.

"Earth could go down this path again. People want to know who they are, where they came from, why evil exists in the world."

"But I can't answer these questions."

"No, but you'll receive the information from the formless realm, the Logos. It will flow through your angelic DNA while you sleep. You are meant to ground the formless into form with your words. There's been a lot of angelic intervention in your life. Your writing will show your gratitude for this help."

That afternoon I buckle Charlotte into her stroller and go to several stationery stores in search of a beautiful book with a gold mandala on the cover and finally find one in Barnes and Noble. It's not precisely a mandala. The image is more like the entrance to a temple with a mandala as part of it, but it is gold on a lovely dark green.

Pushing Charlotte's stroller home I think of Seth. Maybe I should reread *Seth Speaks*. It's been years since I picked it up. Maybe it will help my fear of opening to whatever is in this chrysalis. I unbuckle Charlotte and lift her out of the stroller.

Seth's words float into my head: "Your slightest thought gives birth to worlds. Every single thought is an electrochemical transmission that creates a physical form in some reality."

I hear a voice around my head. "Be the Johnny Appleseed of Light. Plant seeds of light with the information you bring through."

Charlotte looks up at me and smiles. "Johnny apple," she says.

I put my new empty book on my desk and stare at its blank pages. Magic books have blank pages, I think to myself.

While I start dinner I put on "La Bamba," Charlotte's favorite song. She sings along. The phone rings and I turn down the music. It's a patient who wants an emergency session because she woke up in a kind of dream state where she found herself out of her body. I tell her it's OK, that it's a kind of gift and perfectly normal, that it's called astral projection or having an out of body experience. I suggest some books about it and arrange to meet her the next morning.

Exercise: Journaling as the Warrior Path

Buy yourself a beautiful journal. Each night before bed write a few sentences about your day, about whatever's on your mind. Download your worries and frustrations onto the pages. Then close the book. Ask your inner being and your guides to channel information to help you understand any troubling experience from your day while you sleep.

In the morning open your journal and write down any dream or dream fragment you can remember. Even the act of writing a dream down without interpreting it helps your psyche to solve problems, helps you to see your own part in things. A lot of work goes on outside of consciousness when we ask for help. Help is always available from the formless realm, but we must call on it. Discipline yourself to do this as a daily practice. It takes discipline to receive, to hold, to employ what you have received from your unconscious and your guides, so that it will bear fruit.

Chapter 10

Date with Destiny

It's 1998 and Charlotte is four. I still feel sad when I leave her to go to work. I have a new patient, a woman in her early thirties who came last month because she is suddenly afraid of flying. During the past ten years she has flown all over the world for work without anxiety. But for the last few months she's terrified each time she boards a plane. There's no incident she can point to which caused this fear to begin so suddenly. The sudden appearance of this symptom with no apparent cause makes me uneasy. It doesn't have the feel of a normal phobia. I ask her what she has been dreaming, as dreams offer us another perspective on our psyche. Dreams can even see around corners and into the future, I explain.

"I never remember my dreams," she says.

After she leaves our session I meditate. I have the feeling that immediately outside my office door, brushing right up against it, is an ocean. The feeling is so strong that I can't picture what really is there on the other side of the door. Each time I try to remember, all I can see is ocean. I resist the temptation to get up and open the door and look. I sit with the image of the ocean and ask for help from my guides. They remind me that each being has free will and before incarnation chooses events which they want to experience to aid their own or another's awakening. This message rattles me. What does an ocean have to do with this patient? Why am I seeing an ocean right after our first session?

The patient and I work together to help her visualize arriving safely at her destination for each flight she takes over the next several months. This visualization tool was working well until today. She has a flight to Zurich next week and when she tried today to visualize her arrival in Zurich she could not see it and became very anxious. We discussed her cancelling the trip until we can get to the bottom of her fear. She said that wasn't possible, that she had to go now for work. I then suggest she make an appointment with an intuitive in the West Village who is good at seeing agreements that our Higher Self has made which can be causing us anxiety; she isn't interested in this.

After the session I think about her manner as she insisted on taking the flight. It was as if she was saying that it was imperative that she get on the flight, as if it was her destiny. Over the next week she is often on my mind. I call to check on her and catch her as she's leaving for the airport for her night flight to Zurich. She says her stomach is queasy, but she still insists on going.

At bedtime I read Charlotte a chapter from *Wind in the Willows*, and when she falls asleep, I continue to sit there reading on silently to myself until I realize what I'm doing and get up. I look at her little face a moment before I turn off the light. Ali is out for the evening. I wander around the apartment feeling ill at ease. Several times I peek in to check on Charlotte. I get in bed to read but I can't concentrate on my book. I fall asleep to be awakened by a dream.

I'm floating in space in the night sky, far below me is a black ocean, up and up I go, higher and higher in the sky. I see that I'm surrounded by light bodies, hundreds of them also floating up. I'm looking for someone. Then I see my patient and reach for her ankle which is above me in the dark sky. I cannot grasp it. I try again and again but she keeps floating higher out of my reach. I go up higher too but then I'm stopped by a force field, a kind of gateway beyond which I cannot pass. I see many others floating up past me. I am not permitted to follow them.

Ali is asleep beside me. I lie there the rest of the night wondering about the dream. In the morning Ali picks up the newspaper from the doormat in front of our apartment.

He reads the front page aloud.

"Flight 111 to Zurich crashed last night in the Atlantic Ocean just off the coast of Nova Scotia. There were no survivors."

He sees my face crumble. "What is it?" he asks.

Later I meditate and ask my Higher Self and guides why this happened. They explain that every person on Flight 111, before incarnating, chose to die on that flight for their own reasons, many to help those they love to awaken by their death, pain being a great catalyst for awakening.

"That's why you were not permitted to pull her back when you followed her to the after-death realm, witnessed all those on the flight leaving in their bodies and floating in the night sky."

The rest of September passes in a haze. Every day I think about this patient. When I saw that ocean outside my office door why didn't I understand?

October's windy days and falling leaves blow the spiders out of my mind. We plan for Halloween which I have loved since I was a child. Charlotte and I carve a pumpkin together, enjoying the scent as we scoop it out. Ali is away at a conference. Then somehow it's already Thanksgiving, then Christmas and we're in a new year, 1999. What will it bring?

What the New Year brought, what I brought on myself, would not feel good. After sixteen years together Ali and I separate. His lively, positive, rushing about energy is now missing from our home, except when he visits Charlotte. I miss him. What have we done? What have I done? Mongka's words sound in my ears.

"You wall yourself off because you fear your vulnerability. Do you see it, my dear? The spouse is always the hardest test, the last to be loved, always the most difficult obstacle. The highest fence, the great growling watchdogs are always staked out around the spouse."

I sit down on Charlotte's bed next to her to read her the next chapter of her current favorite book, *The Phantom Tollbooth*. We're in the land of Dictionopolis, which is quite close to a place called the Foothills of Confusion. After two chapters her eyelids drift closed. I put the book on her nightstand and gaze at her little sleeping face before I turn off the light. She's only five.

Aimless, I wander around the living room looking for something to distract myself from Ali's absence and my self-recrimination. I pick up *The New York Times*. A new company called Google just launched. It's a search engine developed by a couple of undergraduates in their dorm room at Stanford University. Even though I would normally find this fascinating, the article doesn't manage to hold my attention, and I ask myself again, how did it come to this? A memory floats into my mind. One evening, a while ago now, I said to Ali, "I'm going to lie down on the couch and pretend to be your patient. Will you be present with me then?"

And I did lie down on the couch and tell him how alone I felt. He had nothing to say. He was somewhere else.

I thought love would deepen over the years and create what Jung called "the golden thread," between Ali and I, that it would be our private understanding, that I would be steadfast and loyal. But instead I douched him with a bucket of cold dissatisfaction when I might have been accepting him. A lot of people are dedicated to their work. I knew that about him going in. I broke my commitment again. I try to allow the feeling of revulsion at my behavior move through me until it dissolves, like Mongka has taught me. I see the way I weakened my self-respect by my dissatisfaction with Ali. I struggle not to fall into self-hatred. Nothing justifies self-hatred. You can't banish it from life, but you can choose not to be a slave to it.

Mongka once told me that when you renounce your self-hatred, only love is left. Only the eye of love sees clearly. And on top of that, self-love brings freedom from pompousness. I'll get there.

Now that Charlotte and I live alone how do I grasp my true compass? Where do I step? I wish for a cartographer to make me a map for the next leg of the journey. How do I balance my inner and outer worlds? What will come to light inside me now? Will I finally fulfill my purpose for incarnating? I'm in a scary bit of my life and I want to run. I feel part of me, that part that was Ali's partner, is dead and I have made a terrible mistake. I have failed again. And Charlotte, what have I done to her?

I sit down and cry. I hear Mongka's voice.

"Do you really want to know how to stop blaming yourself and move on? Accept your self-pity. It's alright, my dear. Go on, pity yourself if you must, but understand that you have not yet gotten to the full force of the emotion. You are still in the demolition phase. You will not feel significant improvement until you have surrendered, until you are willing to feel all the wretched feelings that drive you to behave in such self-destructive ways."

Then I really cry. Mongka continues.

"Your arrogance and your willfulness are nothing but your defensiveness, nothing but part of your wall. Your willfulness stops you from doing what you know will bring you happiness. Either you break your addiction to the ego's willfulness, or you will continue to suffer. If you can't, then in the meantime accept your willfulness. Accept your self-pity. You'll suffer less."

I sit staring into space. I feel better after Mongka's visit. I don't want to be alone forever. I don't want to die alone, never trusting anyone, being willful and arrogant, always dissatisfied.

Since age sixteen I have been in partnership with a man, one after another. Born a Libra, a daughter of Venus, I believed that was my path. Jung says that relationship is the path, that our partner is the human being through whom we see God, that the whole Self can only be realized through a human beloved. Psychics and astrologers have told me writing is the path for me, pulling in information from the formless realm to share with other humans. So far I have failed on both of these possible paths.

Over the next six months I turn back to Jung again and again for guidance as I try to understand and forgive myself for the failure of my marriage and breaking up my daughter's home. I examine the archetypes bubbling up from the collective unconscious, archetypes which underpin all human consciousness: mother, father, partner, hero, magician, victim, devil, angel, healer, warrior, king, alchemist, lover, fool, knight, seeker, scribe, monster. I try to see which archetypes I am currently embodying. Certainly mother, fool and monster. I would like to add seeker, but am I a seeker still or have I lost that too?

Looking for another way to communicate with my unconscious I take out my old tarot cards. Although I've used them since college, I've never formally studied them. I sign up for a Tarot Class at the Open Center, which brings me full circle. The Open Center was conceived and born in the ashes of Apple over twenty years ago, when thanks to Zhenya, me and Al, our crooked comptroller, Apple's life was cut short. The Open Center founders pulled the idea from Apple's ashes and ran with it.

A man in the tarot class, Collin, an English writer, born and raised in London, approaches me after the first class.

"Watch out," cries my inner voice when he says he appreciated my comment about The Fool Card, "he's a little too smart and funny and sexy. Don't start eating up his attention and flattery, your ego's favorite banquet."

Collin is compelling and I do dream of the alchemical marriage with a partner, even though I always blow it. Stop wasting time fishing for the experience of being loved, I caution myself.

On my walk home after class I think of Mongka's words.

"The only love you will ever know is in your own heart. Pray to the Creator to reveal that love. It is a prayer that is always answered."

Nevertheless, a few weeks later I go on a date with Collin, the British guy from the tarot class. I eat his compliments and bask in his attention like a lizard in the sun. I rationalize that we share an interest in Jung, in archetypes, and in the world of the unconscious, but I know it's really about lust. God help me.

Exercise: Working with Archetypes

One way to think about what an archetype is, is to see it as a universal pattern of behavior. For example, a hero is one pattern of behavior. A magician is another pattern, as is a king, an outlaw, a lover, a jester, a caregiver, a sage, an explorer, a creator, an innocent, a fool, a victim, a wise woman. Jung believed we all experience these patterns via the collective unconscious.

One way of exploring yourself is to consider which archetype you may be living out and whether this archetype is comfortable for you. For example, if you are the parent of a young child you may love the role of mother or father and feel great ease in it because this archetype suits you. For someone else, staying home with a toddler may be a kind of crucible because the archetype of the caregiver is uncomfortable for them. The provider archetype is a better fit for them than the caregiver archetype. They may long to be out in the world of work and feel stuck and helpless at home with a small child.

Take a moment to journal about the various archetypes you are living out. Ask yourself how you feel in each role. Examine which archetypes are a natural fit and which may have been thrust on you by circumstance.

Chapter 11

Time Wobble

I've been dating Collin for two years. He's moving in with me and Charlotte. I'm uneasy. I know it's a mistake. This is not the way to begin a shared life. There should be more commitment than I feel. Why did I agree to this when I am uncomfortable with it? Why do I position myself across the net from myself? Why can't I be on my own team? Now I'm stuck in it so I'm making threadbare excuses for myself.

"I'm lost in a dark forest," I say to my therapist.

I'm seeking insight, relief, but on a deeper level I'm seeking something still unknown, something numinous which will give meaning to my life, something to stand on, some way to answer the question I have been asking myself since I was six. Why are we all here? Mystics tell us that everyone who takes a human life does it in order to find the Divine within. Instead of looking within I succumb to Collin's flattery and take my seat high up on the dangerous pedestal he erects for me. I deceive myself that we are on a journey.

Summer comes around again, the summer of 2001. Charlotte goes on holiday with Ali, and Collin and I go on what for me is a pilgrimage to Switzerland to visit Jung's home and his tower and meet Jung's grandson, Andreas.

Walking down the path toward the front door of Jung's house I stop. Can I really be here? The image of his house has lived so long in my inner world I can't compute that it's physically real. I stand a minute before the large double front door before I ring the bell. Carved into the stone lintel above the door there's a Latin inscription, *vocatus atque non vocatus deus aderit*. It means bidden or not, God is present. I have long known it was there. Even so seeing it in stone turns my mind inside out as I try to comprehend that something from my inner world is now before me in outer reality.

Jung's grandson lives in the house with his wife. Together they answer the door. They are expecting us. We linger in Jung's consulting room discussing his various artifacts. It's not a museum yet so I can touch things, his desk, his chair, a small lamp, his books. I study the three stained glass windows beside his desk. Then we have tea with them in Jung's library overlooking the lake. I am transported out of time. Will Jung walk into the room at any moment? Is he already here?

The day after our visit to Jung's house we set off for his tower on the other side of Lake Zurich at Bollingen. Andreas has told us that none of the family is there now. The train doesn't stop at Bollingen so we get off at the closest town and walk a few miles along the railroad tracks which run beside the lake. I stop to greet some friendly goats. I must slow my approach to Jung's tower to prepare myself. At any moment it could appear in a clearing or through the treetops. I bid the goats farewell and we continue walking.

Half a mile later there it is, standing behind the swaying branches of a group of tall trees. I stop and stand still. I cannot believe that it exists in the here and now and I am looking at it. Collin turns to see why I've stopped walking, then he sees it too. We go toward it. I am approaching what is for me a sacred space. Jung called his tower a concretization of his psyche in stone, the place where he could be his inner being. We walk closer, right up to it and I lay my palm on it in greeting.

One wall is so close to the lake's edge it's as if the tower is wading in the lake, its feet in the water up to its ankles. It's fitting for the tower to be in touch with the unconscious in this way, standing right in it, as Jung did when he lived, in close contact with both his personal unconscious and the collective conscious. A powerful silence encases us, the tower, and the trees. I feel I'm in Medieval times. This is the home which Jung

85

built out of stone where his eternal Self could live while he was on Earth. And I am here. It feels as if Jung's consciousness is spread out over trees, the land, the water. The breeze has stilled. Only the water moves lapping at the tower's feet. I bend down and run my fingertips through the water. They close around a small stone. I put it in the pocket of my skirt. Maybe it will help me finally write down all the piled-up images from that other realm which crowd my mind. I whisper a prayer to Jung asking for his help to live as he did, expressing my inner being through my human existence, developing my consciousness through contact with my unconscious.

I walk around the tower examining it from every angle, touching its strength, feeling its presence. We sit a while beside it. I don't want to leave. I try to tuck all my feelings into a pocket in my heart. Collin is ready to leave. But my heart won't walk away. My feet are stuck to this ground.

When Jung was in the grip of a powerful emotion he'd look for the image concealed in the emotion, almost like a sculpture hidden in a stone not yet carved. When he found the image he'd focus on it and in that way metabolize the feeling, freeing himself from its grip. So what is the image concealed inside my paralyzing sadness?

"I need a moment," I tell Collin.

I lean against the tower and close my eyes. I ask my unconscious to produce an image to help me understand why I feel powerless to walk away from Jung's tower. I remind myself that my unconscious can produce an image to help me. I feel the tower supporting my back. After some resistance, I see a mountain in my mind's eye.

My inner voice speaks. "Look at it. You must stand like a mountain in the center of your life."

The idea that I can embody the steadfastness of a mountain, which in some sense symbolizes my inner masculine, my inner strength, reassures me. I breathe a little easier. My energy returns. I muster the libido to tear myself away. Jung's tower cannot be the source of my strength. My inner mountain must be that source as it reaches up connecting me to the Divine and downward grounding me into the earth.

"Goodbye, goodbye," I say to the tower as I turn to leave.

All too soon we're back in New York City. It's early September. Time to get Charlotte ready for second grade. My first night back in the city I dream.

I am sitting in a council in the formless realm with beings I know from before I came to Earth. The beings are ovals of light. I am one too. They're telling me a story about human history when suddenly the dream morphs into a blizzard of fire, flooding and collapsing towers.

I wake up shaking, thinking it's about my personal life, that my tower is going to blow up again because I haven't made it of stone as Jung did his. All day I am rattled, unable to concentrate, hanging around outside my body, instead of in it.

A few evenings later I take Charlotte on a sunset boat ride in New York Harbor. While out on the water passing alongside the Statue of Liberty, I look up at the World Trade Center. Lights are just beginning to twinkle on inside. Charlotte asks me something and I turn to her. When I look back the towers are gone. The sky where they stood is empty. I feel a shift like I'm in a time warp, a time wobble. I'm going to vomit. I look up and the towers are there again, lights twinkling. It's September tenth, 2001. What ripple in the atmosphere is this? I tell myself to put it out of my mind, that many stories are carried on the ocean breeze. But the feeling is too strong. To steady myself, I try to concentrate on the smell of saltwater and the feel of Charlotte's little hand as she reaches for mine to ask if I'm OK. I wish the boat would hurry up and bring us back to shore.

The next morning crossing Sixth Avenue as I walk Charlotte to school we see an airplane fly into one of the World Trade Towers. Minutes later the second tower is hit. Charlotte and I stand outside the school with the other families, unable to make sense of it. Then Ali is there beside me, hugging Charlotte. He says, "This is the work of Osama Bin Laden."

"Who?" I ask Ali.

First one, then the other tower falls straight down out of the sky.

Ali has been stopping by each day since the towers were hit to reassure Charlotte who is afraid the Empire State Building will fall down next. Each morning she looks up Fifth Avenue to see if it's still standing. She's six but she understands.

Collin confides that he only feels safe when Ali comes over. What? I think to myself. My current husband needs my former husband's presence to feel safe.

In the days after, as patients tell me their dreams warning that the towers would be hit, I remember my old dreams from twenty years before when I waitressed on top of the towers at Windows on the World.

One patient who worked in the first tower and survived told me that two years prior to the towers being hit his wife had a dream where she saw the planes flying into the towers. At the time she'd been shaken by it but when nothing happened for two years she decided it was only a dream. When the first tower was hit, he remembered his wife's dream and yelled for everyone to get out. He ran down the stairs all the way to the bottom and then all the way up to the Upper East Side without stopping, over a hundred blocks. His wife probably picked up the plan from the collective unconscious at the time Bin Laden was first devising it.

Exercise: Finding the Image inside a Powerful Emotion

When you feel gripped by a powerful feeling, hurt, anger, sadness, loneliness or even when you just feel out of sorts, beside yourself, it's likely that something in your unconscious has been stirred up, constellated, to use Jung's word. That's the time to ask your unconscious, your inner being what it knows about this situation, what it can tell you about this feeling which grips you.

Sit comfortably or lay down. Close your eyes to external reality so you can focus within. Breathe in and out through your nose slowly. Savor your breath. Ask your inner being to give you an image for what you're feeling. Say to your unconscious, "What do you see? Show me."

Then wait until something floats into your mind's eye. Welcome it and focus on it. Don't let your mind distract you with something else. The mind is very good at jumping all over the place and leading you down paths. Concentrate on the image you received. Let it speak to you and show you how it's what you need to see about yourself in order to release the feeling which holds you in its grip.

Write down what you saw. Describe the image. Ask your unconscious why it chose this image. What about yourself is it trying to reveal to you?

Chapter 12

Meeting the Archangels

Someone threw a shoe at Bush's head today. He ducked. We're in the Bush-Cheney years, a shabby time. I attempt to cope with the administration's catalogue of malignant deeds by going to demonstrations and marches. I bring Charlotte with me. Our T-shirts say, "No War in Iraq."

The good news is that I made my final payment on my graduate school loans. The less good news is that Collin and I look out the window and see different views. My friend Carrie asks why I go on with it when there's so much tension between us.

"Staying with him will make you sick," she cautions.

It's a long time since I fell off Collin's pedestal into a ditch. My inner voice begins to stir again urging me to be on my own and write, to develop my own masculine side. I do want to stand like a mountain in the center of my life. By which I mean knowing what I want and doing what I need to do to achieve it. I want to live what I am without bullying myself even while I strive to become more conscious.

I ask my inner being for the gift of a dream to guide me. After a few nights of asking I receive the dream.

Charlotte and I are in a somewhat isolated landscape. It feels like we're trying to escape from something. I see a yellow cab standing in the middle of an empty dirt road ahead of us. Surprised and relieved, I take Charlotte's hand and run toward the cab. I sense something and look up. There is a large Chinese pagoda hanging up in the sky just a few hundred feet above us. It's like it's suspended there with no support. The pagoda is painted green and red. I pull Charlotte along away from it. When I turn back I see the pagoda

*start to slowly slide down out of the sky as if it's sliding down a
mountain, but there is no mountain. We're almost at the cab. When
we reach it I open the door and push Charlotte inside, then jump
in beside her and tell the driver to hurry. We look out the back
window as we pull away and watch as the pagoda crashes down
onto the road behind us, barely missing our taxi as we drive away.
It's like a house slid out of the sky and broke into pieces when it hit
the Earth. It felt like it was coming after us to destroy us.*

I was amazed even while dreaming the dream to see a pagoda
sitting up there in the sky, with nothing to hold it up. Why
a Chinese pagoda? Why a taxi on a dirt road in the middle
of nowhere? What is my unconscious trying to show me?
Our unconscious isn't subject to the laws of time and space;
therefore, it can see around corners and into the future. A
pagoda is such a specific choice. Then the obvious dawns on
me. Collin's mother is Chinese. Because of his British accent
and his appearance, I forget sometimes, that he is half Chinese.
For a moment I'm distracted by the joy of seeing how the
unconscious works, how clever it is in its choice of symbols.
My unconscious wants me to know this dream is about Collin,
that something to do with him is going to fall on Charlotte
and me and crush us both if we don't escape. But the taxi and
the dirt road, what of them? Taxis are how I get home at night
when it's late. They are safe transport. That the taxi appears
lets me know that there will be help, but there's no time to
waste. The empty dirt road may mean that I'm not at home in
this relationship, on this dirt road, and neither is Charlotte,
because where we live all the roads are paved and busy. Or it
may mean that it's the end of the road for me and Collin. The
pavement has run out.

Over morning coffee I share the dream with Collin.

"Yes, our marriage is crashing," he says, ignoring his own
part as the source of the danger in the dream.

The world carries on around us. I try to come up with a plan for separating, but stall. Bush is finally gone, and we have a new president, Barack Obama. I stop to think how many presidents there have been so far during my life. The first president I remember is Eisenhower when I was a child, then Kennedy and Johnson when I was a teen. Nixon and Ford held office during my twenties. When I was twenty-nine Carter was elected. Reagan and Bush, Sr. were in the White House for most of my thirties, and Clinton and Bush, Jr. for my forties and fifties. Now as my sixties begin we have Obama. I've lived a long time already and I'm still asking myself the same question that my six-year-old self asked. What are we all doing here?

In the outer world Charlotte and I go shopping together, plan meals and watch *Gilmore Girls*. She teaches me how to use a computer. Collin is jealous of every moment I spend with her. His jealousy is cold and mean. I know Charlotte suffers from it too. I don't want to do this to my daughter. And I'm supposed to be writing. Stories come to me in my dreams, stories of other beings and other worlds. I feel the words piling up inside my heart. Soon there'll be no storage room left and the doors will blow off. The words of the Minnesota intuitive haunt me.

"If you don't use your spiritual gifts you're going to get sick. Your gallbladder and liver will be affected first because the gallbladder holds our spiritual gifts."

The gallbladder attacks have already begun.

A friend tells me about an Australian shaman, Kerry, the daughter of an Aborigine. Kerry channels celestial beings, including archangels, whom she calls "the Arc's." Sharing her time between the American Southwest, Australia and Peru, she passes through New York City twice a year. Next month she'll be here in New York using a friend's apartment. I book a session with her.

The day arrives. The doorman buzzes Kerry to let her know I'm downstairs. Up the elevator I go to the tenth floor to enter a spacious five-bedroom Upper West Side apartment in a lovely solid prewar building emanating the energy of a bygone slower time.

Kerry leads me to a room where she has set up an altar with drums, feathers and crystals. Outside the window a red-tailed hawk flies back and forth calling to her. Its call is somewhere between a whistle and a cry. We sit face to face. We make small talk while we wait for our vibrations to align. When she reaches the vibration, the band of energy which the Arc's need in order to come through, she presses record. I close my eyes and she begins to channel. I'm already weeping which lets me know I am in the presence of celestial beings.

"The beloved child is here," they begin.

Kerry's voice is somewhat altered as the Arc's use her as an instrument.

"Your soul stretches out into another world. It's time you took on the immensity of that world. We're part of you, beloved child, we, the celestial ones, are part of you, part of your human DNA. We have a direct line to your heart. We want to give you a story. We want you to write it down, bring it into form. Long ago those in the formless realm placed a chrysalis inside you with information for the light beings who have taken on flesh."

I don't realize at first that they are referring to humans here as "light beings who have taken on flesh."

As I listen I feel the joyful welcoming presence of the Arc's and my eyes continually weep.

"It is time for you to open the chrysalis. You are a scribe. Bring this knowledge down and anchor it in the world of form. Shed the distraction and strain of your current relationship. Your vibration is not in harmony with his. His anger is harming you and your daughter. And you needn't take it all so seriously. Eat a cookie. Have a cocktail. Say goodbye to him. We're disconnecting him from you, removing the psychic hook he placed in your womb, your scared space. Slowly we're dissolving the layers of stress from your physical body. It cannot be done all at once. That would shock your nervous system. As we alter your energy field to fill up with joy you will become your own beloved. Understand this process as a supernova of light. You are done practicing with the masculine outside of yourself. You are through allowing others to take up residence in the most sacred parts of you. It is time to focus within. Your words will carry a vibration which brings hope. Bring those words into the world of form. Fling them out like light and plant them on the page. Let them take root. This is your task. Let it be joyful work. Draw on your connection to us, to the whole angelic realm. We will help you open people's minds through story. Those in the formless realm are endlessly feeding you the raw cosmic energy of Source in story form. Visualize us standing around you as you write. Others also stand with you, great scribes from what you think of as the past. You will write a trilogy. You will also write a kind of manual with exercises to show others how to use their intuition, their dreams, and their psychic abilities to help them become aware of their own divinity."

Tears streaming down my cheeks, I vow to myself to do this work.

"We leave you, beloved child, in the love and light of the Creator."

Kerry emerges from the trance state. She has no idea of all she's told me. I thank her and tell her I am grateful to her for connecting me to the Arc's. We sit together for five or ten minutes talking of regular things while we return completely to this realm. She tells me a little of her own journey, her childhood in Australia with her Aboriginal grandmother and mother and her Irish father and of her later work in the jungles of Peru. As I gather myself to leave I feel as if I should bow to the Divine in her, so I do. She returns my bow. I feel a new peace.

The sky opens up and raindrops pelt me as I leave her building. I love it. I take it as a sign that I am being cleansed, that my conscious and unconscious, my greater Self and my ego are coming more into balance. I know absolutely that I am about to begin writing. I feel the words written in the air around me as I walk.

As soon as I get home I look for my empty green notebook with the gold embossed front. I find it on a bookshelf next to Jung's autobiography, *Memories, Dreams, Reflections*. I open it and write down my session with the Arc's. It feels like the most normal thing in the world that archangels spoke to me. It feels like a homecoming. I write that I am ready to open the chrysalis. Tonight I will tell Collin it's over.

He beats me to the punch.

"You know we don't work anymore," he says as we clear the table after dinner. "I've found an apartment. I'll be moving on the first."

He's right, we don't work, but there's more to it. He's fallen in love with someone else, someone twenty years younger than me who is in awe of his genius. I wonder if the Arc's facilitated that. Later as I brush my teeth I think, yes, a young woman might fall in love with him. He's handsome and both wickedly funny and wildly intelligent, just not very full of heart. And he delivers a lot of abdominal pain. At least that's where I felt it for years being around him. I never could digest what he dished out, first his flattery, the ego's banquet, then his cold indifference.

Like many intelligent people who rely heavily on their thinking function, he's deficient on the feeling side. Or as Jung would say, feeling is his inferior function. Our inferior function always has us on a string. Like many intellectuals Collin stumbles over his feelings which sneak up on him and decide his fate. That's probably why he was color-blind for most of his life, and only after five years in Jungian analysis, did he develop his feeling function enough to begin to see colors.

All this is not to say I'm not injured and sad over the breakup. It hurts to be left, even when it's what you want and need. Being dumped for a younger woman makes me feel like roadkill. I want to crawl in between the mattress and box springs to hide. I know it's only my ego that's whimpering. My soul is happy. I turn away from my ego drama and focus my consciousness on my Soul's relief that he's leaving. We've outlived our relationship and we must both detach from it. I must take the sword of truth and sever the connection. "Emancipate yourself," Mongka would say, "cut the tentacles of illusion."

A week later, Collin's movers arrive. Charlotte and I leave and go to the Apple store where I buy my first laptop. That night we celebrate our new freedom with pizza and Mexican Coke. After a decade our home is our own again. The Collin years have ended. It's 2010. Charlotte is sixteen. I put on a Fleetwood Mac song, "Go Your Own Way," and we sing along. Then Charlotte plays "Girl on Fire." We go to bed happy, at peace, safe from crashing pagodas.

Collin has been gone a week and I'm on my way to the bank. I gaze at the different windows with the tellers behind them cashing checks, taking deposits, opening new accounts. Where is the window for refunds on lost time? I'd like a refund for ten years, please.

I dream that:

> I am in my grandmother's house in the bedroom where I slept as a child when we visited her. The bedroom wall slides back. Behind it I discover an entire wing that I didn't know existed. I enter the new space and wander through rooms filled with books and comfortable chairs and lamps and a beautiful study with a large sixteenth century writing table.

These new rooms represent a part of myself of which I have been unconscious. This part of me has been there all along ever since my childhood, even babyhood, days of staying in that room at my grandmother's house. Forget mooning over the time you've wasted. Explore these newly discovered rooms in your psyche. And start writing!

I sit down at my table by the window to write. I hear Beyonce's voice drifting up from a car stopped at the red light eight floors below me. "At Last," she sings.

It's now been six days in a row that I have sat down every morning for several hours to write before going to the office. The words gush out of my pen onto the page in an onrushing stream. Soon I will transfer them to my new computer. I'm still saying hello to it, getting ready to partner.

Exercise: Dream Work

Dreams come from the part of yourself that knows you better than anyone else. Your dreams comment on your life and provide a snapshot of your psyche as it is at the moment. Dreams can also be about world events. Sometimes we don't know whether a dream is personal to us or about the outer world. But most dreams are personal, and everything and everyone in them is an aspect of ourselves.

Before you sleep ask your inner being, your unconscious, for the gift of a dream. Put something by your bed, maybe a journal, that you will see in the morning to remind you to catch the dream upon awakening. It might take some practice. Keep asking. Be patient with yourself. It's worth it. When you get up write the dream down to ground it here in the Third Dimension. Also write down how you felt in the dream and what you think it might be related to. Look at the different symbols the dream uses to speak to you. Carry a symbol or an image from the dream around with you all day, like a little treasure in your pocket. From time to time take it out and look at it and wonder about what it could represent. Ask yourself, why has my inner being chosen this particular symbol? What does it want to show me? What is it trying to say? How do I feel about it?

Chapter 13

Possession by a Dark Shaman

Something is wrong with Charlotte. I'm scared. Suddenly, I mean from one day to the next, she is not at all her usual together solid self. She cannot sleep. She cannot focus. Her eyes are different, frightening, full of terror. Her hands are shaking so hard she can't even hold a glass of water. I don't know what is happening. It feels as though she's in the clutches of a demon. I call Ali. He wants to consult medical professionals. We see four psychiatrists and five psychologists over the next few weeks. We try different medications. Useless. The sleeplessness, terror and shaking continue and now she can't leave the apartment without vomiting on the doorstep. Ali comes over in the evenings. He tries to give her techniques to calm her fear. She can't concentrate. Her eyes are sometimes vacant, sometimes desperate, sometimes someone else entirely leers out at me, threatens me in an alien voice. This is like nothing I've seen before even working on an inpatient psychiatric unit at Bellevue. It feels like we are in the archetypal world in the grip of some demon. She's terrified. I'm terrified too. Ali appears calm. How will she survive this? How will she rid herself of this demon? A broom will not do this time.

I go to the grocery store and on the way home I suddenly know Charlotte is in immediate danger. I run, praying. When I get home she is smashing everything in her room. Broken glass from picture frames covers the floor. Her feet are bleeding. Her eyes are not her eyes. The alien voice says, "You'll be sorry."

"Who are you?" I say to it.

The alien says again, "You'll be sorry. I will have her body or you will see her body hanging from the High Line."

Charlotte neither sleeps nor eats.

Sometimes she speaks for herself in her own voice. She tries to tell me what's happening to her, how she's in a battle with a dark being.

"A black slitheriness crawls over me. It comes at me, I fight it, it backs off. It comes again. It licks my face and chest and spreads a cold mist over me. When the slithering black mist becomes unbearable I crack into a bunch of dark jagged pieces. I can no longer speak as myself. I lose my own voice. I'm not a person anymore. I'm gone. I no longer have a body. I'm somewhere in space with no body. Some dark being has control of my physical body. Later I find an opening, a way to slip back in until it senses me and comes at me again."

I listen to her, holding my breath. Up until now I've more than once wondered how my life was so blessed, so free of major trauma. Now my hour has come. Every moment a prayer is on my lips.

I fall on my knees, "Not Charlotte, please, God."

"What can I do to help her?" I ask my friend Carrie who is a psychologist but also spiritual.

She doesn't know, but she listens with so much love. This is not depression or psychosis. We are in some other realm here. Even Ali, who is a more traditional psychologist than I am, now sees that. I ask my sister Anne what I can do.

She says, "What would Jung do?"

"He would ask his unconscious, his Greater Self, and the collective unconscious for help," I tell her.

That's what I do. I sit still and listen. I try to hear my inner voice. I'm so panicked it's hard to listen in the way I need to. I remember something Jung said.

"It's a great thing to bear a situation that comes to you in life. Then and only then do you discover who you are."

I am so scared. How can I save her? I must find the courage to face this monster with her. I must replace my fear with a will of steel. How is Charlotte going to survive this? She's only sixteen.

I can't leave her on her own for fear of what will happen. I feel that holding her, touching her, even holding her hand, somehow helps. I stop working. I lose my voice. I ask for Divine help, from Mongka, from Jung, from the Arc Angels, from God, from my inner Self. A memory of something Mongka taught me arrives like a gift.

One day before Charlotte was born I was so agitated I wanted to jump out of my skin. Mongka asked me where I felt the agitation. I told him in my whole body but especially in my heart and in my mind. He told me to go to the agitation in my heart.

"Let the agitation of your mind merge with the agitation of your heart, my dear. Don't jam it, drop into it. Get behind it. That's better. When you get behind it, we can shoot the agitation without shooting you as well. Do you see? Sometimes you may have to suffer a wound, but it's not the same when you're not in it. Don't be afraid to believe what is happening. We're making space for you to sit in your heart. We're pulling out a brick. Even at the height of agitation there's always this space of God. Return to it. It's always there. Come home. No matter what is happening or not happening in your life, you can always sit in your heart."

I feel calmer remembering this and I find the space inside my agitation. I sit in the stillness there. I hear the word "exorcism."

I wonder if I should call a priest? Most dioceses still have access to an exorcist, though they don't advertise this. Instead, I contact Kerry, the Australian shaman. She says she can do an exorcism, and a soul retrieval from where she is in the desert. We arrange it.

I also call Cyndi, the healer and intuitive in Minnesota. Over the phone she tells me that a dark shaman in Charlotte's bloodline has died. Charlotte's next in the shamanic line. He wants Charlotte's body. He's refusing to leave the Earth plane. Charlotte's fighting him but he keeps attacking trying to wear her down and she's growing weaker.

"He has a predator consciousness," Cyndi tells me. "He senses her power and he's trying to possess her. The battle is fierce. Her taproot is coming loose from Earth."

I hang up the phone. I'm afraid Charlotte will die rather than give in to him. I cannot let my child out of my sight. I sleep in her room, but neither of us sleeps. I know the world is carrying on somewhere in the background. I no longer know what day of the week it is. Are we in winter or is this autumn or even spring? We are lost in time and space. Our world is made of frozen fear. Nothing moves. I have no voice. I croak or write her notes. She is vacant eyed, contracted in pain.

Kerry journeys to the Cave of Lost Children. A piece of Charlotte's soul is there. It has fled her body. Kerry retrieves it but tells me there's more work to be done confronting the dark shaman, and Charlotte must do it and I must help her.

"Since Charlotte is sixteen, you are allowed to help her in the psychic realm," Kerry explains. "If she was over eighteen you would be blocked by a force field."

The night after Kerry does the soul retrieval I lie beside Charlotte and we both sleep longer than snatches for the first time in many months. I journey to another realm while my body sleeps.

Charlotte and I are clinging to one another, falling downward through worlds of darkness. A half man, half reptilian creature pursues us. He has created a form for himself with a demonic face, a tail, claws for hands, and scales for skin. I try to tell myself he isn't real, that this is a dream. But I know dreams are real, that the unconscious is a fact, that other realms are as real as waking reality. I tell myself he's only a thought form and I can overpower him. But I know even a thought form can possess you. It nearly happened to me on Okinawa. He grabs for Charlotte, tearing at her flesh, lacerating her body even though it burns him to touch her. He attacks again and again trying to enter through her heart, then through her crown. She struggles against him with her will. The three of us tumble downward locked together, falling through worlds, his claws tearing at her hair, digging holes in her scalp. She tries to twist away from him.

I pray, calling for help, "Hilarion, Mongka, Arc's, Sananda, Buddha, San Germain, please, I'm begging for your help for my child."

The beast is up by Charlotte's crown chakra. I know he wants to enter there through the top of her head. I grab him with both hands and yank. I hurl him away with the strength which must have come in answer to my prayer. I watch as he is sucked backwards away from us.

I fly, carrying Charlotte in my arms, to the top of a mountain. I lay her across my lap. She looks dead, her body translucent. I see that her taproot is nearly torn loose from Earth. I rip my own root in half and tie her to the Earth. I feel my hands grow large, I hear Mongka's voice, "Your hands are Mongka's hands." Spiraling emerald light pours from my hands and I know Master Hilarion has come too. I feel their presence as I use the light spirals to heal all the places where the dark shaman has torn her body. A spark of light enters near her heart. It's wobbling around, but it's there. She breathes.

Charlotte is sitting up looking at me. I hear a voice.

"Close she came to leaving this Earth."

I take Charlotte in my arms and rock her to sleep. "Rest now."

I offer prayers of gratitude to Sananda, San Germain, to the Arc's, to God, to Mongka and Master Hilarion, to Kerry and Cyndi, thanking them all. I sit in my heart in the space between the fear as Mongka once taught me to do.

In the days after this Charlotte stops shaking. She begins to draw, abstract work at first which becomes softer as the weeks go by. I watch like a hawk. Yes, she is reclaiming her own Self. My voice begins to come back. How long have we been off the grid? The last time Charlotte went to school was February. It's now August. Eleventh grade ended three months ago for her class.

I consult Cyndi again. She tells me that Charlotte's own soul is back in her body though it's wobbling around. Next I speak with Kerry and arrange to see her when she comes through New York. Over the phone she tells me, "Few are allowed to split their taproot." Before we hang-up she says, "Close she came to leaving this Earth."

Those terrifying words again. How does she know? It's the Arc's, I realize. They spoke those words to me. And they are speaking now through Kerry.

Two months later I see Kerry in person. We align our energies by being together for a few minutes. Then Kerry raises her vibration to a frequency the Arc's can use to come through. She goes into a trance and the Arc's speak to me.

"You sat in the darkest places and bore it with grace while bricks were thrown at you," they begin. "Close she came to leaving the Earth," they say again, and again I feel my heart seize.

"All is well, she will recover. She is a steadfast warrior of the light. Yes, there was angelic intervention, but this is nothing new in your life. You have been held in the field of angelic love since long before your birth as a human. Draw on your angelic connection to help you bring in hope. We are your family. Practice moving your mind at will between worlds to gather secret information and give it form. In a human body you have access to many levels of consciousness. Learn to shift to other levels which are right near your usual state, but which allow for different experiences. Let the process be joyful. Do not fear to be an oracle. It is a responsibility you long ago accepted. There is a conversation going on in the universe. Listen in. Hear the future speaking to the past."

Before I leave, they caution me.

"You weakened your own taproot when you split it. Attend to it by re-grounding. Visualize your taproot sinking down deep into the center of the Earth and spreading small roots in all directions. Do this as a daily practice until you feel your root is strong again. Teach your daughter to do the same. All is well."

I walk for blocks after I leave Kerry and the Arc's. I move along with no effort as if carried on a gentle wave of bliss, at one with all existence and the flow of life, my daughter lives, the presence of the Creator is within me, holding me. The angelic beings are my family. My gratitude is deeper than any words. I never want to lose this feeling again.

Exercise: Grounding to Mother Earth

While we are making ourselves a human body we are also attaching our body to Earth with a taproot. To check that your attachment is strong begin with your root chakra at the base of your spine between your hips and move your consciousness down to the area below your feet and then follow your root down into the Earth. You can imagine yourself on a river flowing down or in an elevator going down or being carried down by a waterfall or riding a spiral of light energy downward. Use your imagination. Go all the way down to the bottom of your root deep inside the Earth until you see your taproot spread out into smaller roots. Whichever way you travel down, bring spirals of light energy with you to nourish your root. Give the light to your root. Thank your root for connecting you to Mother Earth. Feel your connection to Earth. Offer gratitude for the opportunity to be manifest on Earth in the world of form.

Chapter 14

Mongka Revealed

Charlotte is mostly recovered from the attack on her by the dark shaman. Slowly we're re-engaging with the outer world. I check the news to see what we missed during our lost months. I see photographs of President Obama and his team in the situation room as they monitor the killing of Osama Bin Laden in real time. Their faces are deadly serious, terrified that the mission will fail but also both horrified and relieved as they watch the Navy SEALS succeed. I see no hate or anger in their faces. I am reminded of Mongka's words.

"Do you know why Christ said to love your enemy? It is because that is the path to freedom. It is not that you do not fight when it is your duty to fight, but you don't fight out of hatred and anger. You fight out of love. You discharge your duty. When you try to destroy something out of hatred, you're only feeding it life. Hatred is the elixir of immortality to the enemy. When you destroy something dispassionately, out of service, well, it's unspeakable."

We inch along through the weeks back into the world. I watch Charlotte like a hawk. Afraid to leave our bodies, we both still have many sleepless nights.

Gradually over the next six months we recover. Charlotte draws every day capturing her state in a graphic design, trying to understand it, to see it on the page like a mandala to chart her progress. She draws and I meditate. Meditation becomes my salvation.

Mongka's words come to me. "Approach meditation with great sanctity, my dear. When you meditate you are laying the pipes through which grace will flow. The waters of meditation destroy a thousand sorrows. Only meditation can soothe your anxiety."

Finally, I am working again. Charlotte is beginning to see friends again. We're both sleeping. I dream.

I'm standing alone on a wooden platform in outer space. I see that the platform is a basketball court but with no walls or ceiling. It's just an open platform floating in outer space. It has the lines for the free throw area and other circles and lines typical of a basketball court. I look around into the night sky and wonder what I'm doing way out in space alone on this platform. Off in the distance I see the Earth, a beautiful blue and white globe hanging in the night sky. So where am I if that's Earth out there in space? As I watch, the Earth suddenly flips upside down.

I wake up. I know the dream is telling me that my world is about to turn upside down. But how? A day later my sister Anne calls to tell me our father is in the hospital. I cancel everything and rent a car. On the drive up to Ithaca I realize why my dream had a basketball court. Right after World War Two in order to support himself while he was in college my father played professional basketball. Then later he coached many championship basketball teams. But in my dream the basketball court is no longer whole, it has no walls or baskets or scoreboard or ceiling and it is floating in outer space.

I sit beside my father's hospital bed and listen to him breathing. He's slipped time. The temporal world no longer holds his consciousness fast. Untethered, he floats off to other realms. He's entered the eternal timeless world, the world of children and life between life. Sometimes he's in the past of this life getting ready for a basketball game or a football game. Sometimes he's in another realm entirely, talking to beings I don't see. Sometimes he's in this realm with me.

The organized atoms of his physical body are almost disbanding before my eyes, detaching for their journey back to the shimmering world. His consciousness is already roaming the universe. This morning he is back in World War Two on the deck of his ship speaking to his mechanic, asking if his plane is ready for take-off. He was a Navy flier during the war. Yesterday he floated between realms speaking to beings in the formless realm. Now he's talking with his mother, my grandmother, Anastasia, who has come from another realm to escort her son. I cannot see her but feel her. He turns to look at me.

I smile at him through tears. I imagine a dandelion in its ethereal stage, a soft white orb of seeds ready to fly apart at the touch of the wind.

Night falls. Visiting hours are over. I leave. Unable to sleep I look on YouTube for the BBC interview with Jung which he gave the year before his death. I feel like the interviewer cuts Jung off and moves to the next question too quickly. But even so Jung manages to drop pearls of wisdom about the psyche and about death. When they discuss psyche, Jung is clear that humans can slip the confines of time and space and have visions of other worlds and of the future. He explains that we do it every night when we dream but can also do it at will using active imagination.

He tells the BBC interviewer: "Only ignorance would deny this. It is quite evident that this ability exists and has always existed. Psyche is not dependent on the confinement of the body. Psyche doesn't live in time and space alone."

I am filled with emotion watching Jung. His wholeness as a human being breaks my heart open. I want to be this conscious, this whole. I want this for all humans. Then Earth would be a paradise. One day it will be.

The interviewer asks Jung about life after death. Jung is very clear.

"I've treated a lot of old people and heard many of their dreams. The unconscious disregards death. It behaves as if psyche were going on."

Jung doesn't share in this interview something which he recounts in his autobiography, *Memories, Dreams, Reflections*, about his own near-death experience. He describes it like this.

It was as if I were in an ecstasy... the ecstasy of a non-temporal state in which present, past and future are one... where everything that had happened in time was brought together in an iridescent whole.

Restored by watching Jung, I take a bath, say a prayer for my father to experience the ecstasy Jung describes as "an iridescent whole." Lying in bed in the dark I go over what Jung said. Even while we are in a body, part of us lives beyond time and space. Our subtle body is the part of us that continues to exist after we leave our physical body. The Arc's, Seth, Mongka, all say something similar but none of them is human. Hearing Jung speak of life after death in his human voice touches me in a different way, a comforting way. They all break my heart open. I close my eyes and ask for the gift of a dream.

I am in an orchard of pear trees. One of the trees has golden pears. Its roots are coming loose from Earth. It falls over on its side on the ground.

The dream is on my mind as I drive to the hospital. I don't consciously realize that it will be my father's last day on Earth, that today is the day he will be uprooted from Earth. When I walk up to his bedside he looks at me with such love, as he has done all my life. I pull my chair up next to him and hear his whispered prayers, acknowledging the depth of his gratitude to God for creating him. He's always seemed to keep a foot in God's realm.

He turns his face toward me. He's present with me, lucid. "It's alright," he says, "we come from light and we return to the light. I will see you anon."

"Anon," this is not my father's language. I think it must be his Soul speaking.

"Golden angels have come and one of them was called by you," he tells me.

I ask the angel's name. He pauses a moment as if checking, then answers. "Mongka."

I have never told anyone in my family about my relationship with Mongka. This is no unbidden miracle of chance. For the first time in all these years I learn that Mongka is an angel, a golden angel. That's why he told me so long ago that he'd never been a human. How did I not know this? It's nearly twenty years since Mongka offered to be there at the hour of my father's death. How did I never know through all our conversations that he was an angel?

"Of course you've come," I whisper to him. Mongka, whose words, whose love, always bring tears to my eyes, has come. He's here.

Pain grows in my belly as my father, his soul uncaged, moves away from this life. Each breath draws him nearer to the River of Forgetfulness. Soon he'll cross back over it. The indignities of hospital care have ceased. Sensing the slowing rhythm all around him, the staff leaves him in peace. Each moment he becomes less body and more Soul. Soon I expect the bed to be empty save for an oval of light.

My insides hurt. The pain is intense. I go to the ladies' room and crouch down on the floor holding my abdomen. How will I live without the presence of his steady heart? I hear Mongka's voice.

"Your heart cannot hold the pain of so much loss so you push some of the pain down into your abdomen. There is no death. You know this. Your father's Soul has no need of a physical form. Every light being who takes on flesh uses many forms then vacates them."

Despite knowing the truth of Mongka's words, the gut wrenching is so awful it's hard to stand up. "Accept your contraction, your pain—just something more for Mongka to destroy, so that you can know your own Divinity."

I hold onto the sink to support myself as I try to stand. A whoosh of brilliant light sails toward me, encircles me and departs. I know my father is gone from this realm. His inner being is liberated from his body.

It's spring. The days are visibly growing longer but the air is still cool up here in Ithaca. I looked up the poem of the same name, "Ithaka," a few days ago. I feel rather than see Cavafy's words trickle through my fingers.

"Arriving there is what you are destined for. Do not hurry the journey at all, better if it lasts for years."

Today is my father's funeral. I sit in the church with my daughter, my sister, my two brothers, their spouses and children and my mother. My mother has dementia and I wonder if she understands that it is her husband in the coffin. She's silent as a stone, her head bowed. Jung's words float into my mind.

"The Infinite is the only thing which really matters, the only thing which prevents us from fixing our interest upon futilities."

Do I fix my interest on futilities? I look up as if to heaven, as if to find an answer to my question. I see a light, my father I think, floating high up in the rafters overhead. I look at Anne and turn my eyes heavenward. She nods and smiles.

"Yes," she whispers.

Later she tells me, "At his funeral today Dad wanted me to tell you thank you for the cashmere socks you put on his feet in the hospital when his toes were so cold."

Only he and I knew of that. I thank Anne for dropping this little gift into my lap. She smiles her enigmatic smile. I wish I could see her every day, but she lives outside Ithaca on a country hillside among the wildflowers and I live in New York City.

My father's body has been in the ground a week. The rosary of his days on Earth has ended. His consciousness is free to roam the universe.

I am more than halfway through my own life on Earth. Jung believed that for the second half of life we need to change direction and begin sailing inward toward the Self. The first half he saw as a time for sailing outward into the world to make one's mark. Of necessity I will probably work until I die unless I lose my marbles, but that doesn't mean I can't also be sailing inward, reflecting on my journey and listening to my inner voice.

Last night I awoke to find my father standing, not at the foot of my bed as his father stood by his, but by the side of my bed. He looked like himself only a little younger and more translucent. He wore a white shirt with his sleeves rolled up, something he often wore while doing a task.

"I'm ready to help you write," he communicates telepathically.

I want to ask him something else, "What's it like where you are?"

"More beautiful than you can imagine," he telepathically communicates. "Like the most gorgeous perfect day on Earth that you would want for a picnic, but even more joyful."

That's what he used to tell me to imagine when I had a nightmare as a child. I want to weep. He remembers our life. I have so many questions and I'm afraid he'll disappear before I can ask. "Where are you?"

"Space doesn't exist in terms of distance as you perceive it in the Third Dimension. I am separated from you not by space but by something like an energy field. Other environments, including the after-death environment, coexist amid your own

111

but you don't generally perceive them as you are tuned into your own specific reality."

"So you're right here?"

"Sort of. There are mental and psychic energetic barriers, but I can to some extent still perceive physical reality when I choose to focus my consciousness there."

"What happens right after you die? Is there a process you go through after death?"

"Each being's experience of after-death is unique, based on her own expectations and fears. The transition is easier for those who believe in life after death while alive. As we do on Earth, we create our reality in this realm using our thoughts and emotions. But it happens more quickly here since in the after-death frequency time and space are not the root assumptions. In general the laws here are less limiting than in the Third Dimension."

"Is there a life review process for everyone?"

"Before one can know her greater Self and see her other simultaneous existences, she must examine the life just ended to understand that her thoughts and feelings are what created all the experiences she had in that life and also to understand how they affected other people."

"Were you met by people you know from Earth?"

"Aside from your grandmother, I've been more in touch with beings I know from lifetimes other than this last one. Each of us can choose who we'd like to see."

"I want to see you when I die."

"And so you will."

Then he was gone. I lay there a long time absorbing his visit before I could fall asleep. The next thing I knew Charlotte was at my bedside telling me she was off to school. I'd overslept.

Each morning after Charlotte leaves for classes and before I begin seeing patients I sit at my table by the window, put myself in a receptive mode, feel a cocoon surround me and begin writing. I love this time. I welcome the Arc's and those of the formless realm who come to help. It's a group effort. I feel surrounded in a good way. I don't plan. I'm having fun. I write for a few hours letting what wants to come through me materialize on the page. Why did I wait so long to start writing? "Fear," answers a chorus of voices in my head, "but never mind that now."

Charlotte suggests it's time to use my new laptop to write instead of longhand. I don't know how to type but I can learn. She downloads Word for me. I love that it's called "Word." Some inspired human thought to call it that.

Exercise: Reach for Thoughts That Feel Good

Joy is the state of mind which creates the frequency to allow your desires to manifest. We create our lives with our intentions, our thoughts, emotions and expectations. Our thoughts and feelings are magnets drawing experiences to us which match their vibration.

We all get a lot of programing as children and a lot of it is negative and makes us believe we're not good enough. But we can override this programing, if we consciously choose our thoughts. It takes a little attention.

Reach for thoughts which feel good. Find something that makes you feel joyful and think about it a lot. It can be as simple as a parrot tulip or as complex as your long-term goals for your life. Watch the diet of thoughts you're feeding yourself. Give yourself happy thought food. Feel the effect, the change in your state. Use your thoughts to create a feeling of joy within you. This feeling of joy will draw the Divine to you. Practice a little each day to reach for a thought that feels good.

Chapter 15

Life between Life Regression

It's 2013, three years since Collin left and Charlotte fought off the dark shaman, two years since my father died and one year since my mother died. I write every morning before I go to the office to see patients. Things are good.

The phone is ringing. It's my sister Anne. She's just come from the doctor. She has a bladder infection. I don't like the feel of this. Anne hasn't recovered from the deaths of our mother and father. They really knocked her down. I hang up the phone after we speak feeling like someone has just walked over my grave. I hope this is nothing more than a bladder infection. I pray that the ominous rumbling I feel is only the result of the past three years.

I go about my day struggling with my mind which can sometimes feel like a pain factory. My thoughts today are like a herd of wild horses dragging me on hoofs of fear down roads I don't want to travel. Anne, not Anne, I pray as I sink to my knees, the sweetest creature I have ever known, ever since her birth. My childhood partner for watching spaceships over the Ashokan Reservoir, she cannot go on ahead to the next world without me. Journeying to the moon, conversing with garden fairies, looking in the whites of our eyes to see our Souls, these activities with my younger but wiser sister cannot be ending. She cannot be leaving Earth before me, without me. I tell myself to get a grip, to stop catastrophizing. The doctor says it's only a bladder infection.

I argue for a second opinion. For a reason known only to herself, Anne resists this suggestion for precious weeks. Then the bad news arrives. Things move very fast. She bravely says that before she loses all her long red hair, she'll cut it off and

114

glue it to a hat to wear. But it doesn't come to that. Her body can't tolerate chemo. Her white blood cell count is immediately way off in the wrong direction. A brutal surgery fails to stop the cancer. Always slender, in a few months she's down to eighty pounds from one twenty-eight. Her husband orders a hospital bed to be placed in the living room of their eighteenth century house which stands on the side of a hill covered in wildflowers. It's June. Her friends, her daughters, my brothers and I, and her husband of three decades attend her. I sit at her bedside and she tells me she doesn't want to have any regrets when she leaves. She wants to be clear with everyone. She tells us all how much she loves us. She dozes off and her husband and I take a walk in the woods. "I'm madly in love with your sister," he tells me.

The days fall into a rhythm. Anne can no longer sit up or even turn on her side without help. Her friends like temple goddesses attending their queen come every morning to bathe her as she breathes her way toward quietly advancing death. In the afternoon her daughters come to sit with her a while, brush her hair, pick wildflowers for her bedside, clean out the refrigerator, sweep the kitchen floor. Neighbors arrive with casseroles.

At this moment my two brothers and I are alone with her. She tells us how much she loved being a child with us, sleigh riding, raking leaves and jumping in them, winter evenings making popcorn in the fireplace, sitting on the back steps after dinner eating orange popsicles, getting our first Beatles' album. She reminds us of a family trip to Canada and motorboating on the lakes at Thousand Islands.

"I loved that trip," she says.

I never knew that. Three hearts sit there beside her, breaking. It's too soon for her to go.

"I don't want to die now," she says, then adds, "A party, no funeral, just a celebration where nobody steps on anybody's toes."

I nod. She closes her eyes to rest. I go to the woods and fall on my knees beneath a tree. Why is this happening? What agreement did she make before incarnating? This is too fast.

Later I find my brother, Edward, sitting on a stump breaking a small stick into pieces and carefully lining them up. It's a way to show himself that he is breaking apart, that at this moment he's in pieces.

"She's been my best friend forever," he says. "Five o'clock was our daily time. She'd pull into my driveway and we'd sit on my porch listening to Bob Dylan, Neil Young, or some new musician she'd recently discovered, talk about our day."

Edward is so like Dad, I think to myself, steady, gentle, kind, but tough too, with an inner strength. In their world men don't cry. I wish Edward would.

"She's part of the fabric of this little town," he continues, barely able to look at me. "I see her everywhere, driving down Main Street, stopping at the only red light in town, visiting the old people, changing their bandages after surgery, listening to their stories, offering a smile and a dose of kindness, coming out of the post office after half an hour of Mary updating her on her elderly mother's dementia, soothing George's anxiety about his upcoming surgery as he fills her gas tank at the Mobil station, picking up milk and bread and eggs at Clark's and dropping them at Eloise's. She's imprinted on this town."

I know it's a feeble gesture, but I squeeze his shoulder. It's boney with almost no flesh. His pain is harder to bear than my own. Though a grown man, he's my little brother. I ask the trees and air for something new and unexpected to come into his life to help balance the loss of Anne, to help him put his pieces back together. According to Jung that's another way the unconscious helps us. When we lose one thing, one precious person, our unconscious calls something new into being. When Jung lost Freud, Toni Wolff appeared like a miracle in Jung's life. "Dropped from heaven, unasked," is how he described it.

I sit near Anne witnessing the pain and indignity and sublime aspects of her encroaching death. Soon she will birth herself into the next world. I know she already knows this other world well, having partly lived in it all her life, but still a door is closing here. For a moment I remember long ago telling Sophie how sad I was that the door to the other side closed on me when I was two and I knew I had to stay on Earth. Now a door will close again, the other way. And that feels even more painful because I've grown so attached to Anne and to this human world. I've never seen her do a cruel or selfish thing in her life. Instead, as our father told us to do as children, she has lived every day seeing God in everyone and everything.

I see her in my mind's eye. She's high up now, right at the edge of the cliff. If she leans forward only a little, she will fall downward, but only for a moment, before she unfurls her wings. Whose imagery is that? Rilke? Or someone else? The image of Anne standing on the edge of a cliff helps me bear the agony of witnessing her suffering. I see her standing there and know she will soon be free. I focus on the image to block out the picture of her boney form lying on the bed. The image of her unfurling her wings makes the unbearable bearable. Oh, my red-haired angel, yes, you will fly.

Charlotte is outside drawing wildflowers, translating her own emotions into images. We each seem to know that finding the image behind our feeling will help us objectify it, keep it from completely swamping us. We sink down into the emotion just enough to apprehend the pain of her suffering and our loss, and then translate it into an image which objectifies it just enough to make it bearable, just bearable enough to hold.

"Who are all these people in cloaks and brown hoods?" Anne asks me, glancing across the room. Her eyes are almost the only part of her body she can move now.

I don't see anyone, but I say, "They're monks."

"Oh, yes, that's right," she answers.

The invisible and visible swirl through one another as she apprehends both worlds, finding her own images for her journey.

Later that afternoon I sit by her bed reading to her from Michael Newton's *Destiny of Souls*. I come to a passage about the Keepers.

"The Keepers are hooded monks, masters, who restore Souls once they arrive in the spirit world after they have been ravaged by illness," I read aloud to her. The synchronicity knocks me over the head.

"Yes, they're here," she says simply, "and Dad is with them."

I am not surprised to learn this. Aligned with her primordial innocence, Anne had seen ahead through the veil.

By evening, Anne, the house, the hillside, are enveloped in a silent, graceful peace. I kiss her on the forehead before leaving. She reaches for my hand.

"We're all part of the Oneness," she whispers to me.

"Yes," I nod, choking up.

When everyone has left for the day and he is alone with her, Anne's husband pulls their four-poster bed next to her hospital bed and places his pillow so his head will rest next to hers for the night. It's been four weeks since he carried their bed downstairs to sleep beside her.

At dawn she wakes him and looks into his eyes. "I'm going now."

She left on a glorious summer morning. A mighty oak detached from Earth and turned to light. I feel her in the breeze, in the leaves. My brother, Stan, voices my thought. "It's like she's part of the trees and air."

I stand in her garden. A flock of birds circles her house and catches a swift, uplifting rush. I feel what can only be my father's hand on my shoulder reaching me from another realm. I hear his voice inside my head, "Don't hold her on the Earth plane with your grief. Let her go now. Life is forever coming into being and passing on."

Anne and I will not grow old together in this life, continuing our conversation about our children, wildflowers, the cosmos, archangels, our favorite songs. I am bereft. I long to know her experience of leaving the Earth plane and what it's like for her where she is now.

I know there is something called Life between Life Regression because I've read Michael Newton's books. I want to do it and decide to look for a psychologist trained by Michael Newton, since Michael Newton himself has now left the world of form. I will journey to the formless realm and find her and see what it's like and ask her why she left so soon.

I call the Newton Institute and am put in touch with Dr. Aurand. I book an appointment.

A bubbling fountain greets me when I enter Dr. Aurand's office. We talk a little about the process which will be two, four-hour sessions. The first session will be a series of visits to other lives I'm living. I understand from Seth that these other lives are simultaneous with this one even though in the Third Dimension we consider them past lives. During the second four-hour session I will journey to the life between life realm to see Anne.

I lie down on a beige chaise and listen to the fountain. I go into a light trance. For the next few hours we visit other lives that are part of my Over Soul. This is part of his protocol to make sure I won't freak out doing this type of soul journeying. Some of the lives we visit I'm already aware of from my dreams and previous regression work. We agree to meet in two days for the second session.

I arrive and after a few minutes of small talk so we can acclimate our energies to one another I lie down and go into a light trance where I can still hear him and respond. He will keep connected to me with his voice. He instructs me to answer his questions when I'm in the formless realm and to return when he sounds the bell.

He instructs me to go to my most recent death on Earth. I remind myself that all time is now, all things and time are one, so I can more easily focus on it. My inner vision sees that life. I'm a Japanese Samurai. In a detached way I observe as this other aspect of my Over Soul commits Hari-kari and I join with it as it transitions out of the realm of form into the formless realm. It's like my consciousness is riding the coat tails of the samurai just to get over there.

Once there I am greeted by a light being whom I recognize as Jung. I am astounded. This is a gift I wasn't expecting. I know Dr. Aurand is speaking to me but it's difficult to focus on him. My attention is on Jung. I am communicating telepathically with Jung. Trying to explain what's happening in words to someone back in the third dimensional world is a wrench. A feeling of the wholeness of eternal bliss envelops me. It's wondrous. I am floating in the ecstasy of a non-temporal state. Past, present and future are one, nothing is spread out over time. The concept of time does not apply here. Dr. Aurand's voice floats into my consciousness. He's asking me to look down at my form in this realm and describe myself to him. I tell him I'm an oval of blue light. He asks me my name. I say, "Soonam."

I try to make him understand that in this realm and in the presence of Jung's wholeness I can barely find words. They don't use words here. Dr. Aurand insists I hold onto my ego self and the current of time so that I will be able to return to the human world. It's challenging to focus in two realities at once.

Jung understands I'm there visiting and that I wish to see my sister. He communicates telepathically that after I see her, he will return for me.

A purple oval of light floats toward me. I understand it to be an aspect of my father's Over Soul. I am overjoyed to meet him this way. It's so pure, so clear. I'm vaguely aware that my human body which is laying on the chaise back in the Third Dimension is connected to me through an energetic cord. The body on the chaise is weeping tears of joy. Behind the purple oval of light is an orange oval of light. I know it to be one aspect of my sister, Anne. She floats forward and communicates with me telepathically that she knows she left quickly. "It had to be that way—or I couldn't have done it."

I understand her so easily. Communication here is effortless, telepathic.

"My death was meant to be a complete letting go of all attachment. I know I took a harsh road with my physical self to achieve it," she telegraphs. "Letting go of attachment was the lesson I set myself before incarnating."

My father chimes in telepathically, "The Angels cheered for her."

I begin to understand her choice. She had her eye on the long game, the life of her Soul, rather than on just that one life. I'm so happy to be with them in this world where communication is so clear and direct and honest with nothing hidden. They tell me I have a while yet on Earth and many books to bring down from the formless realm before I leave Earth. Anne offers me a book title. *When Every Breath Becomes a Prayer.* There is so much love. I want to stay with them forever.

Dr. Aurand asks me what is happening. I struggle to use words, to straddle both worlds.

Jung is waiting for me nearby. He leads me to an etheric replica of his tower at Bollingen on Lake Zurich. I remember reading that Jung said near the end of his life on Earth that he could already see his "other" tower bathed in a glow of light, the tower which would be waiting for him in the other world after his physical body's death. I am standing beside him in the lake. We are up to our waists in water, facing this other tower. He is shooting light from his fingertips. He tells me to use thought to do the same. I imagine it and the light manifests immediately and shoots out of my fingertips. Things manifest instantly in this world of iridescent wholeness.

"It happens faster here, but we do it on Earth too," he reminds me. "Desire, focus and intention can create physical things in all dimensions."

He emphasizes that humans are creators, "splinters of the Infinite Deity." He explains that the whole physical illusion of material form on Earth is created and maintained by the collective unconscious of humans, that it's a group effort which carries on below the level of our conscious awareness.

"The unconscious is real. It is a creative entity entwined with the Divine," he reminds me.

He goes on to share his current thinking about the anima and animus. Telepathically he reiterates his original conception that the sexes are separated for each life on Earth and one sex or the other remains latent as either an animus or anima within the human. He still feels that the inner opposite compensates the outer gender, balancing it, but explains that he now knows that the reality of the anima and animus is far deeper and richer than he originally supposed.

"They not only represent the Self but they also act as a stabilizing influence for civilization. They carry the Divine aspect within each of us when we are in human form. They help us to keep from over identifying with whatever current physical body we are inhabiting. After many lives as both male and female, when incarnations are complete, our whole Self is then a blending of masculine and feminine characteristics."

We float out of the lake and stand by the tower.

"The sacred marriage of the masculine and feminine," he continues, "which I called the *hieros gamos*, is a problem I struggled with for much of my life. I was trying to show how essential it is to bring together the opposites within oneself in order to be whole."

As we stand there before Jung's etheric tower in this other realm, I absorb his thoughts easily without words being spoken.

Again Dr. Aurand is asking me questions. I am unable put into words the depth of the peace I feel with Jung. I try to share what I can of what I'm experiencing. I struggle to focus my consciousness in two realities at the same time. It feels clumsy to use words. I want to stay with Jung who is now communicating about dreams and how they penetrate the veil of forgetting to allow us to know our whole Self.

"The greatest healer is the Self, the inner being of each human," he reminds me. "Help your patients realign with their inner being, with their eternal man, the Self. This relationship between their eternal Self and their earthly man will be a thorny problem for rationalists who don't believe in an afterlife. Accept each person where he is, at whatever level of consciousness each is capable of and lead him along toward awareness of his wholeness. Begin there, with acceptance of wherever the person is. Help each to live what she is."

I wonder if it was his experience that most patients did achieve wholeness. He reads my mind.

"The majority of my patients came to solve some problem and then went off to carry on with their lives. But some few were destined to go through the whole alchemical process of individuation, to face their shadow and accept it as part of them, then to encounter their inner opposite and unite with it, and finally to create a union between their ego and their eternal Self which is part of the Oneness of all. This is no easy task. The mind must bow down before the heart. A person who goes through this process will meet herself in her Totality. She will be whole. She will know herself as both human and Divine."

Dr. Aurand is ringing a bell. The sound comes from another world. What does it mean? The bell sounds again, more insistently. Then I remember it's a signal. I don't want to leave Jung. I want to stay in this iridescent world with him.

I hesitate to shift my consciousness completely back to the Third Dimension. I know when I do, this world will vanish. I weep in gratitude for my sister, my father, Jung, and all I have learned from them in waking life and here on this visit. They understand my tears as gratitude. Being in the presence of such wholeness is bliss, but I must go.

Dr. Aurand rings the bell again. I force myself to shift my consciousness back to the Third Dimension. I am in my body on the chaise. The other world is gone. But I know the way there now. It's what Anne told me when she was six. You don't will yourself to a place. You imagine yourself there.

I share as many details as I can with Dr. Aurand. I tell him how similar the life between life state is to the dream state. He nods. I share what Jung has taught me. We talk for about half an hour to make sure most of me is back in the Third Dimension. I understand intuitively that a part of the Self is always in other dimensions. Before I leave his office, he cautions me.

"You're too much in the spirit world. You need to ground each day in the Third Dimension. Use your imagination. Picture a waterfall flowing down over a cliff, or the roots of an oak tree spreading out deep inside the Earth."

I walk home stepping deliberately so I don't accidentally space out and walk into traffic. I keep thinking of those on the other side. I hear Jung in my head comparing a human being to the blossom of a plant.

"What we see is the blossom, which passes. The rhizome remains."

On Earth Anne was a blossom, but her Soul always has been and always will be rooted in the eternal world. When I get home—the first thing I write down is the book title which Anne gave me, *When Every Breath Becomes a Prayer*.

Exercise: Practicing Telepathy

This is easier than you think. Back when everyone had landlines and no name popped up immediately on a screen, who didn't sometimes look across the room when the phone rang and know who was calling? Ever had an intuition about something or someone? Ever said to someone, "I know what you're thinking"? We do know what other people are thinking but we block it out most of the time.

Try this. Say to a friend, I'm going to think of an animal or a place, or a song, whatever you want. Tell them not to search for it. Then carry on with your conversation or whatever you're doing. Ask them to tell you when something floats into their mind. Tell them that they don't have to focus on trying to guess because it's not their conscious mind which is doing the work. Their inner being, their unconscious, already knows what you're thinking of and will give them the answer if they don't block it out.

When we engage with it our consciousness expands to include more and more of what was previously unconscious. Each time we integrate new aspects of our unconscious we become more our whole Self.

Chapter 16

A Charming Ghost

It's 2018. Charlotte graduated from Parsons School of Design last year and opened her own design studio. When I suggested that she use her intention and imagination to see clients flocking in and referring their friends too, she said she'd do it the regular way with work hard.

"But one's intention and imagination start a thing on its journey into form, especially if your desire is strong," I tell her.

"My desire to produce creative work is strong, but I'll do it my way," she answers.

I know I should just stuff it. My agitation with outer events makes me feel unbalanced and I talk too much. Things in the outer world don't feel good. It's kind of an off the rails feeling. Trump is on Twitter everyday mangling the truth. It's a real test to keep one's equanimity with him as the loudest voice in the room.

I know I should sit still, stay quiet, and reflect. Let Charlotte follow her own inner wisdom. We each have our own Higher Self. She doesn't need me to tell her what to do. Charlotte and I are different creatures and different approaches work for us. According to Jung's typology she's a Thinking/Sensation Type. I'm an Intuitive/Feeling Type. *Thinking* tells you what a thing is. *Feeling* tells you if something is agreeable. *Intuition* is perception via your unconscious, and *sensation* is perception using the external senses, your eyes, your ears.

I see a strong intuitive function in Charlotte too, but I'm not sure she trusts it yet as she prefers to rely on thinking. And she has a strong tendency to introversion, by which I mean she's more influenced by her inner world than by people and things in her surroundings. I watch her get depleted by too much contact with people. As a more extroverted person I am nurtured by a certain amount of contact with others. No one is a hundred percent anything. We all have some introversion and some extroversion, some thinking and some feeling. Some intuition and some sensation. It's a question of what the balance is.

Sadly, introverts are much underrated in America because America is a young, extroverted country. Charlotte would feel more in harmony in Switzerland which is an introverted country. Despite her shamanic bloodline, she steps around her power rather than into it, especially since the dark shaman attempted to possess her. One day she will take that power with both hands as we all must do. The thing is to give each person an opportunity to be herself. When you have the right relationship to yourself, you are free. That means accepting both your positive and negative aspects, for there's nothing positive without the negative side as well. Everything we are also has it's opposite in us. We are light beings who also have a shadow.

Charlotte comes into my room and sits on my bed. I look up from my computer. "I had a flying dream last night. It felt so great," she reports.

"I love those dreams," I say.

"Are we actually out of our physical body when we have those dreams?"

"Yes, we're in our subtle body which can defy both time and space," I explain.

"Time too?" she asks.

"In the unconscious, time is not a root assumption as it is in waking reality. Because time doesn't exist in dreams or in the unconscious we can be in any time or place, past or future. The dream state is very like the after-death state."

"Hmm..." she says getting off my bed, "I better get back to my office."

By this she means the room behind the kitchen which she has made into her design studio.

I turn back to my writing. It's my joy and sustenance. *When Every Breath Becomes a Prayer* was published two years ago by Deeper Well Publishing. And last year Collective Ink in the UK published *Mission from Venus*. Now I'm working on volume two of the trilogy. It's called *The Wanderers on Earth*.

When I sit the ideas are already in my fingertips like they've been lining up waiting for me to open my laptop so they can leap onto the page. As they come out of my fingers there's a mixing process in which my waking consciousness translates and tweaks ideas coming in from another realm. Sometimes I see words written in the air before my eyes. I say thank you. It's a cooperative approach where guides, my deeper Self and my physical self, all work together. Ideas can also come in from my dreaming Self, which reaches into other dimensions to gather knowledge while my body sleeps. Then when I write, the dream information from my deeper Self, along with the information from guides, mixes with my waking consciousness to make words and phrases. I'm wrapped in a kind of cocoon during this process. It is my sacred space.

I'm not usually aware where I am or what happens in the deepest levels of my sleep, or even what the information is that I'm being given until I sit to write. Sometimes I do remember dreams where I'm not on Earth when I receive information.

If my dreaming becomes lucid when I'm in a very different place in the universe, it still startles me. I know it's not really a different physical place but a different energetic vibration. While my physical body remains in my bed, another part of me is off in a different dimension where I'm being taught and shown things.

As humans we perceive the reality which we focus on. We can shift our focus to perceive other realities. This happens naturally in dreams. There isn't much form in some of the realities I visit during sleep. They're often simply oscillating energy, particles of potential where thought can manifest into things in an instant and communication is telepathic. I love telepathy. It's so simple and direct and nothing is misunderstood or hidden. It will be good when all of us humans use this form of communication all the time because it's so clear. We do already use it a lot without realizing it. And we all have this ability, though it remains latent if we don't develop it. For example, mothers and infants often use telepathy and the mothers may not even be aware of it. A mother may think she simply has a sensitivity to her infant's needs, without realizing that she is picking up her infant's thoughts.

This morning on waking I remembered being in the formless realm learning how our mental acts, our desires, thoughts and emotions create thought forms of us. For example, if you long for someone and imagine you are there with them and you think intensely about them and the place where they are, a thought form identical to you will appear in that place. Although the person may or may not see it, they will sense you. And if they are asleep, they will see you in a dream.

An adept would see you there. If your desire to be there with the person is very intense, the energy of your thought form could carry a part of your consciousness to them. In that case you might see or smell for a second the place where they are. For example, you could smell the apple pie they are baking or the saltwater of the sea if they are by the ocean. When you suddenly think of someone it may be that they're thinking of you and you're picking that up. We humans use mental telepathy a lot more than we realize. We often read each other's minds.

The other thing I remember from last night's lesson is that the guides compared our presence in the physical realm to a firefly blinking on and off. Seth describes this as well. In other words, our bodies are not continually in the Third Dimension. Because of the nature of energy our bodies blink in and out of the Third Dimension. We are in a constant state of pulsation, though we're not aware of this. We are equally here and not here.

That means if you're fifty years old, you've only been here for twenty-five years. When we're not here we're in another reality which we usually block out because our senses are designed for this reality. It's like we're hypnotized by this reality and can't look elsewhere. We don't for the most part even notice these blinks. But if we find ourselves in a daydream, it may be that we're focused on where the blink took us.

Our human body is not the only type of vehicle we have. Even while in a human body, we have a subtle body as well. In other realities, those realities which we tune out, we have other bodily forms and identities, some human or humanoid and some not. Our truest Self is pure consciousness with no form at all.

In the deepest reaches of sleep, where we are no longer in the time bound Third Dimension, we are in communication with our other identities and their realities. Some of this we may remember as a dream, although it will be adapted when we awaken and remember it so our third dimensional consciousness can make some sense of it.

Dreams are of different types. Some are about our Earth reality, some about other realities. Our sleeping self is far more knowledgeable than our waking self, as the Hindus have always known, referring to waking reality as Vishnu's dream.

Dream work is my favorite part of being a psychologist. Yesterday a patient was telling me about a dream where his deceased grandfather was alive again and with him in Trafalgar Square in London. They were feeding the pigeons, happy being together enjoying the birds.

As he was speaking of feeding the pigeons, a pigeon landed on my office window ledge and looked in the window directly at him. We both felt the moment as a synchronicity. Just as he was describing his internal image from the dream, a matching outer event simultaneously occurred, seemingly with no cause, a coincidence, an *acausal* event. When two related things happen at the same moment with no explanation it feels numinous, like there is the presence of something other at work. We both felt it and looked at one another. Synchronistic events often happen when there is a strong emotion present either consciously or unconsciously. Perhaps the power of his love for his deceased grandfather helped to constellate this little moment, this *numen*. A bird is also frequently a symbol of spirit or of the Divine. Birds move between earth and sky connecting them. The patient said he felt as if his grandfather had sent the pigeon to the windowsill.

When he left I thought about synchronicity. Really it's a little creation with no cause. But then, Creation itself has no *known* cause. It just is. The Creator has no cause. The most important cause of all, has no cause. It's hard for my human mind to grasp this. How can this be? Maybe that's why some intellectuals don't believe in God. Rationalists require a cause for everything. How then, I wonder, do they account for synchronicity? Or creation itself? If there's no known cause for creation, how do we happen to exist at all?

There is a less impoverished view of the world, a way of being where the boundaries of the possible are not as narrow as the proponents of rationalism believe them to be. In this wider view it's alright not to have all the answers. It's alright for there to be numinous experiences. Rationalists don't consider that our concepts of space and time might not have validity beyond the Third Dimension. They insist on critical reason as supreme. But life extends far beyond consciousness and reason. The unconscious is real and carries on within us whether we acknowledge it or not.

On my walk home from my office I notice pigeons everywhere. I bring up the mail. Charlotte is out walking Obi so I put her mail on her desk in her office behind the kitchen. I turn to leave and come face to face with the ghost of a young woman standing in the doorway. She is my height and wears a long white dress with a high collar and long sleeves, a dress a woman might have worn in 1900 or 1910. She looks as if she could be strolling the decks of the Titanic. Her hair is piled up on her head in a charming way. She seems at peace as we face one another. She doesn't seem to need or want anything from me. I wonder if she realizes that she no longer has a physical body. Should I tell her and suggest she move toward the light, that someone will be waiting to greet her? She smiles. Is she reading my mind? I wait for her to communicate or to move so I can pass. When she does neither I walk through her into the kitchen.

Ground was broken for this building in 1895 so she might have lived here around the time of the Titanic. She might even have been one of the survivors of the Titanic. Many of those who were rescued from the Titanic were brought to Greenwich Village, to Saint Vincent's Hospital which used to be a few blocks from here until they made it into condos two years ago. I wonder why I've never seen her before as I've lived in this apartment for nearly thirty years. Maybe she is visiting from one of the other apartments. Maybe I was too hasty and should have given her more time or been more insistent on helping her to cross over. I'll see if she comes again. I ask Charlotte if she's ever seen her, but she says no. Unlike cats who take ghosts in stride, dogs are usually afraid of ghosts and run away from them. I haven't seen Obi run from anyone, so maybe this was her first visit to us.

Charlotte and I are both on our own now. Charlotte did have a relationship. But it ended. Relationships are a powerful teacher. We're all a mix of dark and light. You have to swallow someone's dark side to have a relationship with them and they have to swallow yours. That's why our stomachs often get in knots in a relationship like the one I had with Collin. Along with the physical food we eat we are digesting our emotions. Sometimes it's too much and our insides hurt.

I've been alone since Collin left eight years ago. So that avenue of growth through a romantic relationship is closed off now. But I'm not really alone. I feel the daily presence of the Arc's and Mongka when I'm writing, and of others in the formless realm too, my guides, angels, Seth, Ra, Jung, my sister, my father. More and more as I grow older I appreciate what Jung said when he was in his eighties. It was something like, when one is older one has a quiet relationship with one's books and one's writing.

Yesterday I had a session with Kerry, the Australian shaman, and the Arc's came through and greeted me so joyfully, "The beloved child is here."

They addressed my writing first. "There's an endless fountain of information in the formless realm for you to reclaim and bring into form. Write it in the form of a story. And include information about dreams. It is the dream world which supplies the energy and vitality for your physical world. It is the dreaming self who teaches how the vibration of love creates the photons which sustain your physical world. The dreaming self is also a problem solver. Many humans already realize this. Why else do people say, 'Let me sleep on it'?"

Abdominal pain from the Collin years still comes and goes. The Arc's address that next.

"Every physical ailment has its origin in the emotional baggage you're carrying, which usually comes down to the mistaken belief that you are not loved. Watch your thoughts. Refrain from negative thinking, refrain from judgement of others and from self-judgement, then the energy that you were allowing to flow negatively through you will gather strength and break the obstruction inside you which is causing your physical pain."

I thank them for their help.

They continue. "When you feel dark or heavy or angry, find someone or something and give them love. Love literally creates photons, light. The greatest protection and healing is always love. Love is a state of consciousness which you can choose."

Next without my asking the Arc's speak of my sister, Anne.

"Your sister is playing out in the celestial light near the Andromeda Galaxy. She moves between worlds. She sometimes visits you when you're writing and drops ideas in the chalice of your ear. Are you aware of her?"

I tell them I am. But I miss her physical presence in my world. At her death my grief ravaged me like an onrushing invader hollowing me out into an infinite ache. Visiting her in the formless realm during the life between life regression eased the ache.

"It is your writing which eased your pain," the Arc's tell me reading my mind. "You well know your sister exists as an eternal being of light. 'Dead' is just completely unfocused in physical reality. If humans would shine, they must be polished. The polishing was too strong for her body. When a purification, a polishing, is too strong for the body we call it death."

Then they change the subject.

"Humans are no longer completely Homo Sapiens. They're becoming Homo Luminous. A neuro reboot is happening in humanity. The carbon-based human bodies used in the Third Dimension are becoming crystalline-based bodies for life in the Fourth Dimension. This is the hour for humans to claim their divinity. Everything is malleable though it doesn't appear so in your reality. Events don't 'happen' to you. You materialize them using your attention and intention. Love creates photons. You use photons to create your perceived 'physical' reality. It is humans who use love and light as building blocks to create and form matter by directing their attention to what they want and intending for it to exist. It is not a matter of luck. It is a matter of what one intends. Be conscious of your thoughts, intentions, desires and emotions. They are the vibration-creating-tools which wield love and light to create everything."

Before I leave, the Arc's remind me, "No matter what happens, maintain your equanimity. No matter what the crisis, you are cradled in the arms of God."

Exercise: Enlisting the Help of Your Own Unconscious

Lie down on your sofa or yoga mat or your bed and close your eyes. Let your mind empty and begin to drift. If you're full of thoughts, try breathing softly through your nose into your heart. Imagine your heart expanding, absorbing the sips of breath like a sponge absorbs water. Then let this image go. Allow yourself to drift into a fantasy. Fantasy is a bridge which can unite your conscious self with your unconscious. Jung compared fantasy to a waterfall which unites the conscious world at the top with the unconscious at the bottom of the waterfall where the water strikes the earth.

Allow a spontaneous fantasy to arise or choose an image from one of your dreams. Focus on it. Give it your full attention, allow it to go where it wants, give it a free hand to transform as it wishes. Watch what unfolds without interfering as if you're half hidden, peeking out from behind a bush or door, watching. Stay with it, actively observing it.

Jung called this process active imagination. Seth calls it blinking into another reality. Afterward, write down what you've experienced to ground it. Let it work on you. Discern for yourself the message inside the vision.

Chapter 17

Ra

In the outer world it's June 2022 and Joe Biden is president.

I haven't written for a few days. When I miss too many days of writing I get out of sorts. Writing keeps me in balance, in touch with my inner being. Like meditation it creates the pipes through which grace can flow. Mongka said repeatedly that for a balanced person no situation is emotionally charged. I'm not there yet.

Getting riled up emotionally hurts our bodies because our physical health as humans is dependent on our subtle energy. Lots of things affect our subtle energy, world events, our work environment, our family atmosphere, our relationships, and most especially our own thoughts.

There's an activity for each of us which brings us back into balance. Maybe it's playing an instrument or gardening or taking a walk, singing, running, painting, hugging your dog, feeling love for someone or something, comics, lilacs, lavender ice cream, your baby, or your cat. Whatever opens your heart will open your channel and bring you into harmony with your inner being. Our inner being is who we really are—a divine light-being temporarily housed in flesh. When we're in touch with our inner being our health is better, we're happier, more in balance, peaceful.

Even though we are living on a small planet way out on the edge of one spiral arm of the Milky Way Galaxy and there are 250 billion suns like ours in this galaxy alone, we are far from insignificant. Mongka once told me that humans are the crown jewel in the Creator's crown. I was surprised he would say this, as he usually counseled against arrogance and pretension.

Today I'm re-reading Ra's transmissions in *The Law of One*. Ra is a sixth dimensional being who contacted Carla Rueckert in Louisville, Kentucky, in 1981.

Ra, like Mongka, the Arc's, Seth and Jung, is one of the beings I turn to again and again for guidance. Each of them offers a greater understanding of the relationship between our eternal self and our human life. They are my main teachers even though none of them is now incarnate in this dimension.

Ra, Mongka and the Arc's all agree that in every infinitesimal part of each of us resides the Creator in all her power. They also agree that the Creator resides in all life forms but humans have the capability to become conscious that we are creators. Like snowflakes, each one of us is an individual, a unique expression of Source. I try to remind myself every day that each of us is a treasure valued beyond measure.

But our uniqueness, our individuality is a delicate plant. In order to stay awake and keep evolving each of us must keep our individuality from getting smothered and tarnished by too much society, too much education, sophistication and pretension, too much identification with big groups. Too much group identification crushes a person, morally and spirituality, because we can shirk responsibility and hide in the group. When we push responsibility for our actions on to the group we dilute our personal responsibility. When we act alone, we must take full responsibility for our actions. It is this owning of our responsibility which makes us better humans. But in order to protect our morality and individuality we must live in a free society. Some societies and all cults have a ruthless disregard for the individual. In them no one is free, every person suffers and feels diminished. When individuality is stamped out, we are all worse off.

Jung pointed out that the bigger a group or a cult becomes, the less intelligent and rational it is, and therefore, the greater its capacity for violence.

You can see this phenomenon now in America with the radicalization of the extremes. As part of a big group, people's individuality is smothered. In a group of thousands any one person can more easily feel emboldened to speak and act in ways which threaten the lives of others who disagree with them. In a big group we can forget to love. Reason goes out the window. We don't take time to reflect on what we're doing. Reflection shows us what is unique in us, what is individual in us. It shows us the special way the Divine manifests in us. When you lose your identity to the group you also lose your awareness of your divinity.

As I write I'm remembering the words of my Jungian analyst from years ago, who's now long gone to another dimension. He used to say, "Sparrows fly in flocks, eagles fly alone."

Liz Cheney is at the moment showing the courage of an eagle. I think about her and the price she is willing to pay for speaking the truth as I put on my sandals and grab my sunglasses to go for a walk with our dog Obi.

When I return I give Obi some cool water and flop on the sofa to recover from the oven-like New York City summer heat. I pick up *The Law of One* again. It's also called *The Ra Material*. When I first read it, it upended my life in a good way. Ra gave me so much understanding and hope. He came closer to answering the question of my six-year-old self, *what are we all doing here*, than anything I'd so far read or experienced. Or maybe I was finally ready to hear.

Ra first spontaneously spoke through Carla Rueckert on January 15, 1981. The other two members of the team receiving Ra's messages were Don Elkins and Jim McCarty. Don asked Ra the questions. Jim recorded the sessions using a reel-to-reel tape recorder. Carla was the instrument Ra used to speak. At the time I was in graduate school in New York City and unaware that this was happening or how important it would be to me years later when it fell into my hands, literally.

In the first session Don asks Ra to tell them who he is and what his purpose is for contacting them. Speaking through Carla, who is in a trance, Ra answers.

"We are of the Law of One. We are not a part of space and time, but from a vibration where polarities are harmonized, and paradoxes have a solution. Our vibration of unity is our identity."

Ra explains that he is a social memory complex from the Sixth Dimension. I imagine this to be a kind of multi-self-being. Seth who speaks from the Fifth Dimension says something similar about his Over Soul, but Seth still seems identified with one personality. Ra doesn't seem to have a self which is separate from his group identity the way Seth does. Maybe this is one difference between fifth and sixth dimensional beings.

Ra tells them that he evolved on Venus millennia ago when Venus was a sixth dimensional planet. He says that he visited Earth and even walked among humans in a shimmering golden humanoid body eleven thousand years ago during the time of the pharos but has not returned here in a body since that time. At that time Ra traveled to Earth by means of thought. He manipulated the intelligent infinity (the Divine) present in each particle of light, each photon, so that he could create a replica of himself visible in the Third Dimension. He explains to Don that photons are the building blocks used to create all matter.

Don questions Ra about how he was free to come here 11,000 years ago when there was already a quarantine around Earth. Don seems to know that beings from other parts of the universe are not permitted to just visit Earth. Ra tells him that permission to come must be granted by the Council of Nine, though some beings do manage to slip through the quarantine around Earth. The Council of Nine which is responsible for this part of the galaxy, Ra explains, resides in the Eighth Dimension in Saturn's rings. It was they who granted Ra permission to come to Earth eleven thousand years ago.

For this communication with Carla, Don and Jim, Ra is not on Earth. He is communicating information through a narrow band of energy open between the dimensions, using Carla as the instrument to express himself and answer their questions.

My mind wants to explore the idea of these dimensions and who is in which dimension and what type of consciousness each dimension supports. Don asks a lot of questions about this and it's fascinating to me. I remember thirty years ago asking Mongka what dimension he was speaking to me from. He didn't tell me; instead he counseled against focusing on this kind of information.

He said, "All these dimensions are creations of the mind, a sort of catalog the mind imposes on the Ultimate. You cannot find the truth by grasping for it outwardly. Look within to purify your mind. As your mind becomes purified you will be able to see what order there is in the universe. As God reveals herself to you, she will also grant the vision of her beauty and organization. When the mind is purified nothing is hidden."

Despite Mongka's admonition my mind still tries to comprehend the way the universe is ordered and constructed and how it works and why we're here. Ra and Mongka and the Arc's completely agree on the biggest thing—they all say the universe is One Being, and we are each part of that being. All three also stress the importance of meditation for reaching a state of higher consciousness and contacting our Higher Self. They all consider silence the key to open the door of the mind so it may be used as a tool to understand the heart.

But they each feel a little different to me when I am in contact with them. They are each unique. Ra is methodical, precise, emotionless, a little like a wise all-knowing machine who wants only to be of service. Ra's consciousness is single pointed on the overarching concept of Unity, the Oneness of all things, The Law of One. Ra never gets riled up. But he has certain rules about what he will divulge. If he believes that certain information would transgress on the free will of another he will not share it.

Mongka, on the other hand, is definitely not a neutral machine-like being. We have a personal relationship. He is a taskmaster and a wordsmith, a poet. His goal is to polish my soot-covered diamond soul by pointing out my shadow. He can be hard, telling me of my pretentiousness, pettiness and controlling behavior, my backstabbing and dishonesty. But when he softens to commend my progress I fall apart into tears of love. We are emotionally intimate. He knows me in my totality.

The Arc's, though intimate with me like Mongka, are never critical of me. They never try to polish me by pointing out my shadow. I guess they know Mongka has that covered. The Arc's are joyful, openly loving and tolerant of me. Or maybe I am less frustrating now than I was when Mongka started working on me thirty years ago. I've only been consciously aware of the Arc's since 2011, whereas I met Mongka in 1992, when I was more pretentious and fuller of ego. Whatever the reason, the Arc's don't shine a light on my weaknesses. They mostly encourage me to use my writing and to remember why I came to Earth. They remind me that they are my family, that I am a Nephilim. They tell me often to call on them for help. They also say things like "don't be so serious, enjoy your human body. Eat a cookie, have a cocktail."

Does anyone use that word, cocktail, anymore, I wonder. They are probably using the vocabulary of the shaman and that may be a word she uses.

But back to Ra. As Don asks Ra questions and Ra answers using Carla's voice, Carla is in a trance and knows nothing of what is said.

Ra explains that there exists a complete Unity which connects everything, a Oneness. He tells them that the universe is infinite, and that infinity is Unity. Everything else, right and wrong, good and evil, dark and light, is a misunderstanding of the complete Unity which binds everything. All these dualities are only teaching tools for the Third Dimension. In higher dimensions all duality is resolved and good and evil do not exist.

This reminds me of the feeling of wholeness and oneness I had when I visited the life-between-life realm. It's challenging to grasp this information rationally with the mind. You have to feel it. It's a feeling of peace and bliss, not simply believing, but rather knowing that ultimately all is One sublime divine whole. I reach toward Ra's message with my heart, at last feeling I understand why I am here, why all of us are here. We're meant to wake up in the Third Dimension and get the message that we're all One, we're all Creators. Each of us is creating our life moment to moment.

This reality is finally sinking in now I'm in my seventies. It must have been trying to sink in all my life, but I wasn't ready. How patient Mongka had to be with me. How loving and patient the Arc's are. From age six to your seventies is a long journey in one way, and just a flash in another. This question of who we are and what we're doing here on Earth has been with me the whole journey. Mongka and Seth and the Arc's, my father, my sister, shamans, intuitives, Jung, my dreams, all pointed the way. Ra is part of this line of magnificent beings who have accompanied me through this lifetime, and perhaps other lifetimes as well, watching and guiding and teaching me. Ra provides a glimpse of the big picture which gives me peace and hope.

Maybe I could still see this big picture as an infant, probably I could, probably we all can, before we are hypnotized by the camouflage of third dimensional reality. But the task, the journey, is to wake up in the camouflage, stop judging ourselves and all those around us, and remember that we are Divine Creators creating our lives. Every one of us does it, either consciously or unconsciously. That's the answer I have been seeking all my life and it's so simple. I'm here to wake up and know that I too am Divine and so are you. Everything is OK. In the end we all wake up.

Consciously knowing ourselves as Divine, how should we live? What should we do? For starters Ra says, never infringe on the rights of another. That's not as simple as it sounds. Because everything is another, every blade of grass, every nail, every flower petal, every photon. At least we can be aware of this as we live our days. We can acknowledge the Divinity of all beings, animate and inanimate. I think I knew it as a child but lost it along the way. We can also forgive ourselves and everyone else too. Forgiveness stops karma.

Ra gives Don guidance about connection with the Divine. When you open a pathway to Source, to the Divine, it allows you to know who you truly are, a Divine being, pure consciousness without form. At your core you are love. A connection to Source is what allows you to heal. It opens your heart chakra, your Green Ray Center and ultimately your Violet Ray Center.

"The simplest manifest being is a photon," Ra tells Don. "Every photon is God."

As I read this I remember Master Hilarion directing me to use Green Ray light to heal my toes as a child when I froze them. He told me to use the light of the Green Ray and to imagine myself wearing an armor of light to protect myself from the shape shifting reptile-man. He said to be like the knights in King Arthur's court only with armor made of light, and that healing happens when you remember you are part of God and that God can do anything. If you are God, then you can do anything. He said the best protection I could ever have is to remember that I, and everyone else too, even the scary reptile-man, is God.

"Ask the God in you to make you an armor of light," he said.

Now I see that Ra and Master Hilarion offer the same message. Master Hilarion gave me the answer I was looking for, but I didn't recognize it. At eleven, I was both too old and too young and too scared of losing my toes, to grasp what I might still have understood at six.

Don likes to ask Ra about the pyramids. Ra says he constructed the pyramids using thought. He created the Great Pyramid using thought about 6,000 years ago as an aid to help humans toward enlightenment. The other pyramids were constructed later using local earthly material, rather than thought-form material. But now the time of the pyramids is past, he explains. They are no longer in the right alignment to help humans awaken.

I'm less interested in the pyramids than I am in knowing more about how we can all wake up and know who we are and what comes next. On this subject Ra explains that the illusion that we are alone and separate is what creates so much pain for humans. Meditation, prayer and contemplation can show us, help us to understand, that we're not alone and separate, that we never were. He says to accept responsibility for each moment—that each moment contains love. Ra also talks about how we progress up through the dimensions to become more and more conscious on our journey back to Source.

He says this is an auspicious time on Earth. It is the time of Earth's ascension into the Fourth Dimension. All of us here on Earth can enter the Fourth Dimension along with Earth if we can hold enough Violet Light to survive the vibration of the Fourth Dimension. Once you get there, Ra explains, the Fourth Dimension is much more loving than the Third Dimension which is full of struggle, full of the tension of opposites and conflicts.

Carla, Don and Jim are beings Ra calls Wanderers. They don't remember that they're Wanderers until Ra tells them. Because when we pass through the veil of forgetting at birth, we lose all knowledge of our greater self and memory of where we came from. Those are the laws governing incarnation on Earth. In 1981 when Ra spoke through Carla, he said there were 65,000,000 Wanderers living on Earth. There are probably more now. Wanderers come here to help humans wake up and make the transition to the Fourth Dimension. Ra says the true home of most of the Wanderers now on Earth is the Fifth Dimension. They volunteered to come here to help us wake up and remember that we're Divine beings so we can make the leap to the Fourth Dimension along with Earth. If you're reading this you may be a Wanderer yourself.

Because Wanderers must pass through the veil of forgetting too, just as humans do, and then wake up and remember who they are, and that they came here on a mission to help, they can't help us wake up until they wake up themselves and remember their mission. If they don't wake up, they'll get stuck in the Third Dimension. It's a risky mission they have undertaken.

Those in the formless realm who guide my writing directed me to write about Wanderers. They probably put *The Ra Material* in my hands too.

Ra explains that there are two main paths and we each choose one, either the path of *service to others* or the path of *service to self*. Some love the light. Some love the dark. Those on the dark path of service to self are after power, especially power over other people. Those on the light path of service to others are seeking to help others. If you observe, you can see the choices people have made. Mother Teresa and Gandhi chose the path of service to others, but you don't have to be that all in. Being a parent, a nurse, a bus driver, caring for a pet, are also ways of being of service to others, as is smiling as you pass someone on the street, or holding the door for the person behind you. Cheating another person, seeking power, seeking to control others, infringing on the free will of another, are acts of service to self. Ending someone's life is the ultimate power you can have over them. We're mostly all a mix but it's about where the balance lies. Are we mostly about service to others or mostly about power over others?

Ra says that we can progress as far as the high Sixth Dimension on either the path of *service to others* or the path of *service to self*. After that only the path of *service to others* will take you forward. At that point everyone jumps onto the path of *service to others*, because at this level of consciousness there are no others. We are all One, all part of the Unity, part of the "many-ness" of Infinite Intelligence, part of the many-ness of Source. I'm so looking forward to this state. I think our Higher Selves are all already there and they reach back to help us.

Now that I understand that we all came into the Third Dimension to learn that we're all One, I see that the information has been there all along and it's everywhere. I just didn't see it. In Mongka's terms, my mind wasn't purified enough to grasp it. All along it's been in my dreams, in the information from the formless realm, in stories and myths, in Seth's books, in messages from the Arc's and Mongka, in Jung, in the writing of the ancients and the poets, and the mystics and in the words of Jesus and Buddha, among others. Millions of humans, billions even, before me have found the answer to the question, *what are we doing here*. I'm following in their footsteps.

What if Miss McGinnis, back in first grade in the 1950s, had given me a different answer to that question. What if she had not said, "Aren't you a Christian?"

What if instead she'd said, "We're here to wake up and remember that we're each a spark of God, we're all Creators, creating our lives. And everything, every beam of light, every nail, every piece of chalk, is also a spark of God. We're all made of the same light. We're all made of photons and love. Everything flows from the Divine mind."

That would have made perfect sense to my six-year-old self, to most people's six-year-old selves. Then we'd all get a jump-start on awakening. It would have been such a relief to know that. Back then I was closer to my true self, before the tarnish, soot and grease of self-judgement and judgement of others covered my spark. At six I would have happily accepted the idea that I came to Earth to be a creator. Most kids are open to fantastic ideas. Some babies still know the truth of who they are, if any memories manage to cling to them after coming through the veil of forgetting. By later childhood a lot of knowledge about who we really are is gone as the camouflage of third dimensional reality has pretty much taken over, unless you're like Carla Rueckert or Jane Roberts and manage to keep a channel open so someone like Ra or Seth can come through and show you the Creator's plan.

It's so simple. We're so powerful. Each of us. It gives me goosebumps. We've been given the ultimate gift, the ability to create using our own thoughts and emotions and desires. We can each open a pathway to the Divine. Healers and psychics do it. Edgar Cayce had his pathway open and was in direct communication with Source.

In Ra's words, "We are all creators, and each of us can open a pathway to the Divine."

Can you imagine a greater gift than this? Ra gives Don a list of things each of us can do to open our pathway to the Creator:

Seek love in every moment.
See everything as One being.
See the universe as One being.
Gaze in the mirror. See God.
Look at another. See God.
Gaze at all creation. See God.

Ra explains that when we meditate we help these ideas sink into the roots of the tree of our mind. Besides meditation there is other help available to us. One being we can ask to help us is our own Higher Self. Our Higher Self operates from the Sixth Dimension. In that sense our Higher Self is our future self, who we will be when we're conscious that we're in the Sixth

Dimension. But while we're in the Third Dimension our Sixth Dimensional Self will help us and guide us. But we must call on it. We must ask for this help or higher beings are not allowed to intervene. So, ask.

Exercise: Contemplate the Idea of Yourself as a Creator

In each infinitesimal part of ourselves resides the Creator in all its power. Let this sink into the roots of your mind. Contemplate it. Imagine yourself as a Creator. Imagine the magnitude of this gift which we all have, the ability to create our lives as we would have them be.

As you go about your day remind yourself that you are an eternal being of light. Seek love in every moment. Each morning gaze in the mirror. See the Creator. When you meet someone else, see the Creator. See the Creator in everything.

The first effort is daily spiritual practice. Dedicate a few moments to quieting your mind each day.

The second effort is relentless inward-looking, self-inquiry, scathing self-honesty. It's precisely what we're unable to see about ourselves that hurts us, controls us.

The third effort is vigilant remembering that you are a Creator. Merge your mind into the Divine Mind. Merge into the light of a thousand suns.

When you approach your life as a good time, life itself is play, life itself is worship.

Chapter 18

Astral Projection

It's October, my favorite month. In a few weeks I will turn 75. I'm not sure if that is considered old. I don't feel old. Certainly 75 is the evening of my life. Jung compared the course of human life to the course of the sun. As it rises in the sky in the morning it grows stronger and stronger until high noon when it reaches its zenith. Then the descent begins and the sun moves steadily downward in the sky, its rays growing softer, less intense until it disappears below the horizon at sunset. Even though I am on the descent, in the evening of my life, I want to make it as meaningful as the morning.

I live a simple life. Aside from a few friends, my daughter and my patients I don't see many people. What I love is a quiet conversation with my books, Jung, Ra, Seth, Emily Dickinson, Walt Whitman, Tolstoy, Rilke, Rumi, Byron, Neruda, Jane Austen, Emerson, Yeats, Khayyam, Homer, Heraclitus, John Donne, Hermann Hesse, Swedenborg, Dante, Charles Schulz, too many others to list. I don't want to die of mental starvation, after all. I owe a debt of gratitude to all of them.

More and more I seek solitude and the company of my guides and my own unconscious as it speaks to me through my intuition and dreams. What can I at this stage of life still desire beyond a right relationship between my inner eternal Self and my outer human self? To be in right relationship to my whole self, I must continue to investigate who I am, to look at what is in my shadow, at what I am keeping hidden from myself about who I am. By now I've learned that it's what I don't see about myself that hurts and controls me.

Animals are natural and real. They live what they are. I want to be like them, living what I am and not putting on airs. I want to be natural and real and not chew on flattery and lap up compliments. I observe my dog, Obi. He always leans toward love, even if he's never seen the person before. No one is a stranger to him. He has a consistent attitude of welcome. When someone returns his welcome, it's transformative. It's alchemical. I want to welcome people that way too. And I want to do my work with a humble spirit and not get sloppy and inflated by flattery. When you live who you are, you are naturally of service to others. I've set myself the challenge to be authentic and welcoming.

I've been here in Greenwich Village for most of the last fifty years, since I was twenty-five, with a little timeout living in Berkeley. New York City is my home, the place where my roots go deepest into the Earth. I love my apartment on Fifth Avenue and Ninth Street, but the rent is through the roof after thirty years of steady increases. Other things are expensive here too. Life would be more economical almost anywhere else. As I approach 75, I'm contemplating moving.

Charlotte wants to move to Marbella on the southern coast of Spain. I do want to at least be in the same country as she when she marries and has children. So I may be uprooting myself and moving somewhere else for the final leg of my current journey in the Third Dimension. But there are other people to consider. Will seeing patients only on Zoom be OK for them? If I move far from my sister's daughters who have no mother will they feel abandoned? And how will my brothers feel? Can I sink new roots into different soil far away from New York City? Will they take? Each night I ask my inner Self for the gift of a dream to speak to me on this matter of uprooting. So far I've been drawing a blank.

Last evening just before sunset I went to the Whitney Museum. As I stood outside in the warm late summer breeze on the top deck amid the outdoor sculpture, overlooking the Hudson River on one side, and the High Line and Greenwich

Village on the other, I felt a heartbreaking love for this city. How can I say goodbye to you? How can I thank you for these fifty years? How can I show my appreciation?

My inner voice whispers, "Just feel it. The city will understand. And write down what you want for this next leg of your journey. Send it out to the universe like a message in a bottle. Allow the universe to work on it. That way it will be a perfect unfolding whether you move or not."

What do I want for this final leg from 75 to maybe 85 or even 90? To start, I love the seasons. I especially love autumn and winter. Marbella where Charlotte wants to go has no seasons. I want to be someplace with seasons and space around me. I would love a small patch of earth to garden. And, I want to be near Charlotte. I want to work and write and live with animals and maybe people or a person.

"Things are already shifting, falling into place," my inner self assures me. "You're not going to end up heartbroken, alone and living on raw turnips."

As I walk home from the Whitney through the Village weaving through street cafes filled with what looks like mostly twenty-something diners sipping wine and laughing, I see life renewing itself. A minute ago, it seems, I was a twenty-something living in New York City. New life is always pouring in and I will be making room by leaving. Others will sit by the fountain in Washington Square Park, put their arms around the trees, walk their dogs on Village streets, visit the lilacs and fountains in Central Park, walk the halls of the great museums, check out the latest restaurant, watch the sun set over the Hudson River.

Jung would never have abandoned Swiss soil. Will I be at peace uprooted from American soil, living as an ex-pat. I love America.

If I'm to make the right decision about the next leg of my journey, there are conversations I must have with myself about who I am and how fruitful my voyage has been to this point.

Have I grown enough over the course of my seventy-five years? By this I mean am I a more conscious human, or to use Jung's term have I *individuated* to some degree, have I owned my own shadow, become conscious of my inner beings and their world and tried to balance that inner world with outer reality. How deeply do I know that I am a creator, a divine being? Does my persona, the mask I wear as I function in society as a mother, sister, aunt, friend, psychologist, author, neighbor, allow space for my greater Self, the Divine in me, to breathe through it? Have I sufficiently unwrapped the constraints of my persona so that I am real with others rather than a stiff cardboard cutout or a pompous phony?

And on the other hand, have I harnessed my fantasies, my intuitions, and made use of them while not allowing them to swamp me so that I am useless in the outer world. Have I spared myself too much self-criticism? Have I been relentless enough in examining my dark side, my personal evil, my contribution to the collective evil? Where am I still pretentious? Long ago when I was still a girl, Mongka warned me.

"When surrender is scarce, pretension walks in. Humility leads to awareness. Humility opens the same door which pretention slams, locks and mortars shut."

Have I grown enough to be humble? Not quite. I still catch myself judging others because I have not completely severed the tentacles of my own self-judgement. And along the way I have hurt people. Anyone can see these surface things about herself, but what about more subtle evil. I must dig a little deeper to find and uproot that.

I'm a long way from the summit of self-knowledge. But I am trying to see the self behind my mask. I'm not the naïve unconscious girl I was at twenty-five when I arrived in New York City or the six-year-old asking her teacher, "What are we all doing here?" But just how different am I from them? Have I done well enough? How much of this lifetime have I wasted?

Am I grateful enough for this auspicious opportunity of a human life?

Turning 75 and thinking of leaving New York City has set off a self-evaluation which is due at my time of life anyway. In her seventies one is no longer venturing out on the high sea, but journeying homeward, to use another of Jung's metaphors.

I will devote some time each day to these conversations with myself. Then I will ask my greater Self and the universe what I should do. I will cast that message in a bottle into the great cosmic ocean and see what it comes up with.

At least I'm writing every day now. Something just occurred to me. Back in 2010 the Arc's told me I would write a book, with exercises, a kind of manual or guidebook to help others work with their intuition and their paranormal abilities. Maybe this book, the one I'm writing at this moment, the one you're holding in your hands, is the book the Arc's were talking about.

Charlotte is seeking a deeper understanding too, as she struggles with the decision about moving to Spain. At twenty-eight she's still sailing into the morning of her life, on the rising arc of her journey. I worried at first when she suggested moving to Spain because she's an introvert and introverts fear the unexpected. When something happens unexpectedly it rattles most introverts. They don't shift gears easily. Introverts need time for their inner being to process a new situation. In a move such as this there will many unexpected situations. Yet her determination is so strong that her inner being has tried on several occasions to take over the reins and push her caution aside. For the first time she's conscious when she's astral projecting. Last week she came into my room to tell me a scary experience she had during the night.

I woke up in pure terror—on an island in the Mediterranean. I was convinced I had fallen asleep on a chaise on an island in the Mediterranean Sea. I jumped up from the chaise completely disoriented. I was in a cabana type thing but with a locked gate. I feared that I would have to wait all night on the island before the gate was unlocked. I tried to unlock it, but I couldn't. I went into problem solving mode. Then I saw my computer on the chair in the corner of my bedroom and my body across the room lying on my bed. I was terrified. How can I be looking at my body across the room? If I'm not my body, who am I? Who is this self that is somewhere else looking at my body? Who is trying to unlock the gate?

Since last week Charlotte has had two more out of body experiences. Each time she found herself by the Mediterranean Sea without her physical body. Though this experience of becoming conscious without her body terrified her at first, she now understands that we all leave our bodies every night when we sleep and even when we're taking a nap. She wants to know more about both astral projection, which is also called an out of body experience, and about lucid dreaming. Astral projection and lucid dreaming are easy to confuse and can occur together.

When we have a strong desire to be someplace or with someone far away, a part of our psyche sometimes travels in our subtle body to that place without our physical body while our body sleeps. If we wake up and become aware that we're somewhere different from our physical body, then we're having an out of body experience. We all leave our bodies every night, but we usually don't wake up during this. If we do wake up while out of our physical body there is a distinct feeling of return and reconnection when we reunite with it.

Lucid dreaming is something else. Lucid dreaming is when we realize during a dream that we're dreaming. When we have conscious awareness while we're dreaming that we're in a dream. Imagine becoming conscious while in a so-called "unconscious" state. In a dream we're in a place without time; we're in the eternal now. When we become lucid while dreaming, we can alter our dream experience to some degree. If we happen to be flying in the dream, we can choose which direction to go in, for example. Or we might be able to open a lock, which we can't do during out of body experiences where we've projected our consciousness to another place through astral travel.

You can learn how to make your dream lucid, and how to astral project. There are classes using some of the same techniques Seth used to teach Jane Roberts and Don Juan used to teach Carlos Castaneda.

When Charlotte consciously acknowledged to herself the strength of her desire to live on the Mediterranean Sea, her inner self stopped astral projecting to be there. Now that her conscious ego-self is trying to figure out the logistics of a move, her inner self has calmed down. Her inner self understands that she has made her desire clear to Charlotte's conscious self and that her desire has been heard.

You may think it strange that there is another within you who has her own desires, her own point of view, but there is. The unconscious is a real place, where other aspects of us live. These aspects of ourselves can give us information which is not available to our conscious self. Because the unconscious self is not bound by time and space, it can see around corners and into the future. Psychics use this aspect of their inner selves to move freely into what we think of as the future. They understand that since time is only real in the Third Dimension it's just as easy to remember the future as it is to remember the past when you enlist the deeper self who lives outside of time. The reason psychics aren't one hundred percent accurate is that free will exists and free will enables the creation of multiple possible futures. Even before we take an action our thoughts alone create many possible futures. Psychics can only tell us the most likely possible future. Each of us can develop the ability to use our unconscious to "see" the future.

Exercise: Meeting Your Inner Selves

Lie down and close your eyes. Breathe gently through your nose. Let your breath take you by the hand and lead you into your heart. Allow this little time of stillness and focusing within to refresh you. Imagine that your unconscious is a landscape, a sea, a forest, a desert, a garden, whatever comes to you or whatever landscape you most enjoy. Fill in as many details as you like. Look around and see if anyone is there in this landscape. Be patient. Invite your inner self to come to you. When a being shows herself or himself, acknowledge this being as an aspect of your inner self. Invite it to tell who it is and why it has appeared. See if it has a message for you.

Our inner figures are often guides who can teach us and give us information. Their consciousness is not bound by time so they can tell us what's likely to happen in what we think of as the future. When you finish the exercise write down your experience of the beings you met. Also write down messages they had for you. This will ground the meeting in your third dimensional reality, in the here and now. Writing in a beautiful hardcover journal can be a good way to honor these inner beings. This is a little time to be with your inner self. The whole of life is encapsulated in one's relationship with herself. How deeply do you love yourself?

Chapter 19

There Is a Conversation Going On in the Universe

Charlotte and I are in Marbella. I fell asleep last night listening to the Mediterranean Sea roll in to sweep the shore. The sound rocked me to sleep. This morning I awakened to the same steady sound. It drew me out of bed, right to it, almost as if it was talking to me, welcoming me. Welcome transforms an interaction into a celebration, a festivity. The sea welcomes me and I welcome the sea. We begin a conversation. We acknowledge that we're both part of the bigger conversation going on in the universe. I listen to the voice of the sea, allow it to calm me, wash away layers of stress. Though the sea is constantly moving, it nevertheless evokes a stillness in me. I walk in up to my ankles, my knees, my waist, my neck, then lift my feet from the sea floor and swim out beyond where the waves are breaking. I am floating, held, lifted-up then set back down with each wave.

Sitting on the shore drying off in the sun I remember how I once sat as a young girl on the shore of the South China Sea more than fifty years ago. Today is my 75th birthday. Yesterday a realtor showed us several homes for sale in Marbella. None felt quite right for us. I see how at peace Charlotte is here, yet somehow, she now seems less intent on moving here. Maybe to come and stay a while each year would be enough. Perhaps it's that the reality of leaving all her friends in New York has tempered her desire to move and live by the sea, even to be in a place she feels is her natural home.

It's also, I think, that she sees that this man who lives here, the one who opens her to a greater state within her own heart, is on an inward journey and an outer partner could be a distraction for him. Maybe their time together is in some other lifetime. He does not pursue her, to make her "feel loved." He does not give her the transitory "feeling of being loved," rather his presence puts her in a state where she experiences the love that is her own being and his. She becomes more porous. I see the last remnants of any brittle defenses fall away when she is around him. In his presence her eyes overflow because her own heart unfolds. This is a different species of love than the "feeling of being loved" by someone. It is a kind of Grace, a love of the Divine resting within everything, which this man evokes in her. And yet practically, in this world, she senses that a romantic relationship with him would not work. She lists him in her phone under family. She is sensible, realistic, practical.

Do I speak with her of love? Do I say, everyone who takes a human life does so to find the Divine resting right in her own heart? Everything else is circumstance, as Mongka would say. When Charlotte talks of the heart-opening state this man awakens in her it feels like the remembrance of some other life together.

By choice she has been single for the past five years. Now she feels ready. And a new man has appeared in New York who she feels could become important to her. Whichever partner she chooses the goal is the same, as it is for all of us—to dive headlong into the deep well of love in our own heart. I long to say, oh, don't let one day go by without tasting the great love within you. Don't settle for fishing for the "feeling of being loved," it's transitory. But she's twenty-eight, an adult who must make her own choices.

I stay silent and I look to my own state. I fished for the feeling of being loved for more than fifty years, at least for a lot of that time, allowing myself to be led this way and that by my ego, not conscious enough to direct my own will. But thankfully, along the way I encountered Master Hilarion, Mongka and Seth and the Arc's and Jung and Ra and a bunch of obstacles which were really opportunities for me to wake up and attempt to demolish my pretentious ego. Now for a decade I have not fished outside myself too much. I spend a little time each day diving into the fire in my own heart. At least for a few minutes I keep this appointment with the Divine. No matter what my mind is telling me I need to do, I try to surrender to that place in my heart where the Creator lives, that place which dissolves all questions, the unified field from which everything comes.

As far as working on myself, I'm still in the demolition phase, trying to demolish my ego, crack myself open, extend through my vulnerability to destroy any remnants of my arrogance. I hear Mongka's voice—a memory remembered from before Charlotte was born:

"At last you've cracked. Now we can all rejoice. It's so beautiful when the ego cracks its veneer of composure. A certain combination of inner and outer pressure is necessary to accomplish this. And then the auspicious moment."

Mongka was always good for supplying the outer pressure. He once told me, "You're not very nice sometimes. But you don't see it. You're afraid of having your raw nerves, your meanness, your hysteria unmasked. It'd be so humiliating."

I did feel humiliated when he said that and I cried in shame. But he stayed with me. He told me he was right there.

"Where?" I asked. "Where are you?"

"As close as your breath, mostly closer," he answered. "Breathe into the humiliation. Allow the hysteria to simmer away. Keep giving birth to greater and greater experiences of yourself."

That conversation was thirty years ago. I don't know how much time I have left in this life to finish this demolition work on my ego. I better get on with it and allow Charlotte to find her own path.

But then again as a mother I want to share everything I think I've figured out about life that might be of value to her. I have to remind myself that Charlotte has her own wisdom, her own knowing. I resolve to keep my nose out of her business and focus on my own state.

I close my eyes and lay back on the beach. I feel the warmth of the sun on my body. I imagine it burning away all my ignorance and fear. I ask the sun to light a fire in my heart and I dive into it. I see the fire in my heart become a pillar extending in both directions, down through my spine and up through all eternity. I give myself to the fire. The heat in my chest eases my breathing. I float inside the fire. I am the fire. I feel a kinship with all things, the sea, the rocks and sand, the sun itself.

I return to our balcony overlooking the sea where Charlotte has arranged freshly squeezed orange juice and croissants and cappuccino. She wishes me happy birthday. Together we listen to the waves brush the shore.

She goes for a run, then a swim, then returns to the balcony which stretches the whole length of this large apartment, to do her own work. She sits under the yellow and white striped canopy covering the balcony and types on her laptop. I sit apart also on the balcony, reading, writing a little, staring at the sea, listening to the waves. The day goes by in blissful peace. In the evening we walk the three miles along the beach to Old Town. The sky turns lavender. Golden light sweeps the sea. Always we are listening to the waves.

I understand Charlotte's longing to live here. I understand why she astral traveled here when she left before. I wonder if that will happen again when we leave Marbella.

On our last night we have dinner with the man who evokes such love in Charlotte. I feel his energy. I feel the energy between him and Charlotte, the watery, oceanic connection they share. We are sitting by the side of the Mediterranean Sea in a small, beautiful, serene restaurant with no walls between us and the water. A gentle misty rain is falling. The sun has set. I can extend my hand out and feel the misty drops. But we are sheltered, dry and warm.

We are exchanging ideas. He speaks of light and at that moment lightning fills the sky and strikes the sea, lighting up its whole surface. A synchronicity, a numina. We three marvel at the universe. Again lightning strikes the sea. Is this doubling of the lightning meant to remind us that his journey to the light is the mainspring of his nature? And that human passions can only be preliminary to this for him? Still, beneath the surface I sense feelings between him and Charlotte which could ignite like fire in a dry field.

He and I talk of his ideas and mine. We share a love for San Germain, Master Hilarion, Jung, too many beings and ideas to mention. We go on talking in soft tones accompanied by the sound of the sea. Beneath my conversation with him, he and Charlotte carry on a silent conversation, heart whispering to heart.

We all have too much to share to fit into this one evening. But that's all we have, this one night. Now and then the two of them come up from the depths in their hearts to share a laugh about something. I am filled up. After dinner the rain has stopped. They go for a walk beside the sea in the mist. I go back to pack but am drawn out to the balcony. The sky is festooned with stars. Jupiter is the brightest thing in the sky tonight. For a moment it looks back at me. I linger on the balcony.

Our week on the Mediterranean is over. We drive from Marbella to Malaga then fly to Paris where we board a plane for JFK and home. Too soon we're back in Greenwich Village. I wake up to the sound of the waves on the shore. It's so real I'm confused about where I am. I want to continue my conversation with the sea. I want to keep hearing its voice. Charlotte astral travels back to Marbella the first few nights we're home. Each time she wakes up across the room from her physical body. She's caught between two worlds.

Our New York life welcomes us back, begins to absorb us once again. New York speaks in a different voice, but it has its own alchemy, offers its own welcome. It's also part of the conversation in the universe.

I take Obi for his bedtime walk and look up at the sky. There's Jupiter shining down on us. I love New York. I love the Mediterranean Sea. New York City has been my home for fifty years, but I think I can live anywhere. Nothing will be decided as quickly as I thought. I relax back into New York, receive its welcome. Welcome draws welcome from another.

I keep writing and seeing patients. Soon this book will be finished. I feel the end of it not far ahead. I'm sure I've forgotten to include something. But, it's OK. When it's done, I'll let go of this voice, my most personal voice. I'll return to writing Book Three of my *Mission from Venus Trilogy*. I've missed those beings in that book, Soonam, Lord Sananda, Maepleida, San Germain, all of them really. I wonder what they're up to. It's nearly time to give voice to them again, to let them speak.

We've been back from Marbella for two weeks. It's Halloween. This morning the streets are full of little kids on their way to school in their Halloween costumes: fairies, elves, dragons, superheroes, ghosts, ghouls, ballerinas, baby pumpkins. My mother loved Halloween as much as we did. Her excitement made it even more fun for us. When I was eight she made me an angel costume for Halloween. It was my favorite costume ever. Even as an eight-year-old I saw how much work she put into it, fashioning the angel wings out of wire which she covered with a white gauzy material. She was a wild horse who frightened me as a child, but she was also a magician. Events and holidays came alive at her touch. I offer a prayer of gratitude to her for this.

I realize now that she did me another service I never recognized while she was alive. She kept my ego in check, kept me from getting "too big for my britches." I was always nervous around her, fearful of her judgement. She had a lot of little sayings like, "Those who live in glass houses shouldn't throw stones." Usually her sayings were pointing out my ego, some fault of mine, like judging others, or stubbornness or insisting on being right. As a little girl her comments felt to me like poisoned arrows. But they were more deeply supportive than I knew. I now understand that one must give the boon of strength, bear the abrasion of the embarrassment and humiliation of being reprimanded and exposed in order for the impurities to be buffed away. Much later Mongka put it like this: "There's great freedom in humiliation and tears."

When we see our stubbornness, our willfulness, our defensiveness, we become a little freer. Mongka told me once that intelligent people have pride of being right. You can either die being right or die knowing God.

"Develop a distaste for being right, my dear," he said.

He also said that "the ultimate deal would be to get enlightenment without ever having to confront your ego, but this deal does not exist except in your fantasy. Enlightenment, in fact, is the continual awareness of the ego. Understand that the ego has been entrusted with the creation of suffering, that the mind is a pain factory."

These days I feel Mongka very near and so I weep a lot, tears which dissolve the layers of fear. For so many years my fear of looking deeply at myself, the good and the bad, insulated me from the knowledge of what we're all doing here. Finally, I get it. I came here into the Third Dimension to wake up and remember that we are all Divine Creators. That's why we all come.

Using our attention to focus, and our intention to transform, we can create whatever life we desire. In fact, our desires are already there in the unified field waiting for us. We must use our attention and intention to enter the unified field, the Divine mind, and take hold of them. Our own spark of divinity can guide us there.

Everyone who takes a human life does so to discover that they carry a spark of the Divine within them. Just as we are, we are all Divine. Our ego tries to keep this a secret from us. But it's true. Everything else is circumstance. It took me all my life to understand this, but now I do. The answer was in me all along. We are all creators. We are all Divine. Our essence is pure being. At the deepest level of reality, we are pure consciousness floating in a sea, a unified field of energy. This field gives rise to all forms of creation, including each of us. Now I see that. And it's such a relief. It's pure joy.

Even though it's November the fountain is still on in Washington Square Park. Rainbows continue to form everyday right through the upward shooting water. The park gardeners are doing the fall planting, putting hundreds of tulip, crocus and daffodil bulbs in the soft earth. Life renews itself.

I've been editing this book, the one you are reading, for the past few weeks, tweaking it here and there. I spend a little time with it each day after my morning visit to the park with Obi. This morning we saw them bringing the Christmas tree on a long flatbed truck. They're putting it up under Washington Square Arch as they do each year. The tree lighting and caroling will be a few evenings from now. The spirit is growing. I feel love from strangers in the street. It's as if it flows from an infinite source, which it does. I offer a silent blessing to everyone I pass. I wish for everyone to feel the great bounty of the cosmos which is there for all of us.

As I write these last few words, I wish for you, wherever you are, that you may awaken to knowledge of your true identity as a Divine being, a Divine creator. Embrace this bliss, even knowing that you're a scandal. We're all a scandal, and despite that lovable just as we are. Make peace with yourself and feel joy in your own being. Accept yourself as a creator. That's all any of us came to learn. Thank you, dear reader, for taking this journey with me. I've learned more about myself from talking to you.

One Last Exercise: Fire in the Heart

Breathe into your heart, softly. Savor your breath. Feel the fire in your heart. Allow the fire to grow bigger and warmer with each gentle breath. Watch the fire extend to become a pillar, a pillar of pure fire down through your spine and up through your crown to all eternity. Give yourself to the fire, feel its protective healing warmth. Let it burn away all separation from your true Self, your Divine Self. Feel the purification as you dive headlong into the fire. Let it burn away all your fear. Let it burn away all ignorance, all prejudice, all your judgement of yourself, all judgement of others, all separation from Love. Throw it all in the fire. Allow this Divine Combustion to burn away everything that separates you from the Divine Light which you are.

It's time for me to say goodbye.
Goodbye, goodbye.
Love,
Susan

ALL THINGS PARANORMAL

Investigations, explanations and deliberations on the paranormal, supernatural, explainable or unexplainable. 6th Books seeks to give answers while nourishing the soul: whether making use of the scientific model or anecdotal and fun, but always beautifully written.
Titles cover everything within parapsychology: how to, lifestyles, alternative medicine, beliefs, myths and theories.
If you have enjoyed this book, why not tell other readers by posting a review on your preferred book site?

Recent bestsellers from 6th Books are:

The Scars of Eden
Paul Wallis
How do we distinguish between our ancestors' ideas of God
and close encounters of an extraterrestrial kind?
Paperback: 978-1-78904-852-0 ebook: 978-1-78904-853-7

The Afterlife Unveiled
What the dead are telling us about their world!
Stafford Betty
What happens after we die? Spirits speaking through mediums
know, and they want us to know. This book unveils their
world...
Paperback: 978-1-84694-496-3 ebook: 978-1-84694-926-5

Harvest: The True Story of Alien Abduction
G.L. Davies
G. L. Davies's most-terrifying investigation yet reveals one
woman's terrifying ordeal of alien visitation, nightmarish
visions and a prophecy of destruction on a scale never before
seen in Pembrokeshire's peaceful history.
Paperback: 978-1-78904-385-3 ebook: 978-1-78904-386-0

Wisdom from the Spirit World
Carole J. Obley
What can those in spirit teach us about the enduring bond of
love, the immense power of forgiveness, discovering our life's
purpose and finding peace in a frantic world?
Paperback: 978-1-78904-302-0 ebook: 978-1-78904-303-7

Spirit Release

Sue Allen

A guide to psychic attack, curses, witchcraft, spirit
attachment, possession, soul retrieval, haunting, deliverance,
exorcism and more, as taught at the College of Psychic
Studies.

Paperback: 978-1-84694-033-0 ebook: 978-1-84694-651-6

Advanced Psychic Development

Becky Walsh

Learn how to practise as a professional, contemporary
spiritual medium.

Paperback: 978-1-84694-062-0 ebook: 978-1-78099-941-8

Where After

Mariel Forde Clarke

A journey that will compel readers to view life after death
in a completely different way.

Paperback: 978-1-78904-617-5 ebook: 978-1-78904-618-2

Poltergeist! A New Investigation into
Destructive Haunting

John Fraser

Is the Poltergeist "syndrome" the only type of paranormal
phenomena that can really be proven?

Paperback: 978-1-78904-397-6 ebook: 978-1-78904-398-3

A Little Bigfoot: On the Hunt in Sumatra
Pat Spain
Pat Spain lost a layer of skin, pulled leeches off his nether
regions, and was violated by an Orangutan for this book.
Paperback: 978-1-78904-605-2 ebook: 978-1-78904-606-9

Astral Projection Made Easy
and overcoming the fear of death
Stephanie June Sorrell
From the popular Made Easy series, Astral Projection
Made Easy helps to eliminate the fear of death through
discussion of life beyond the physical body.
Paperback: 978-1-84694-611-0 ebook: 978-1-78099-225-9

Haunted: Horror of Haverfordwest
G.L. Davies
Blissful beginnings for a young couple turn into a nightmare
after purchasing their dream home in Wales in 1989.
Paperback: 978-1-78535-843-2 ebook: 978-1-78535-844-9

Readers of ebooks can buy or view any of these bestsellers by clicking on the live link in the title. Most titles are published in paperback and as an ebook. Paperbacks are available in traditional bookshops. Both print and ebook formats are available online.

Find more titles and sign up to our readers' newsletter at
www.6th-books.com

Join the 6th books Facebook group at
6th Books The world of the Paranormal